MY JOURNEY DOWN
THE BIG MUDDY

Love, Heartbreak and Triumph
Jet-skiing the Mississippi River

Bill Ayars
with Susan Valerian

Instant Publisher
P.O. Box 340, 410 Highway 72 W.
Collierville, TN 38027

Copyright © 2015 Bill Ayars and Susan Valerian

All rights reserved, including the right to reproduce this book
in whole or parts of any form.

Designed by Staci Buck and Natalie Ata

Photos by Bill Ayars and family and Susan Tarry

Manufactured in the United States of America

ISBN: 978-1-61422-914-8

To Jennifer and Jackie

CONTENTS

Map		9
Foreword		11
1:	Big Muddy, Here We Come	15
2:	"You Don't Know How Close to Death You Were"	23
3:	The Seaweed Debacle	36
4:	Phoenix	49
5:	Back On The River	59
6:	Susan Recovers, We Keep Going	68
7:	Move the [Bleeping] Barge!	79
8:	Jennifer Opens Up	86
9:	Rocky Ride	96
10:	Mud Man	101
11:	We Made It, Baby! Almost . . .	111
12:	A Light in the Night, Then Screams	118
Final Chapter:	Time to Celebrate and Reflect	127
Sources		135
Acknowledgments		137

OUR JOURNEY

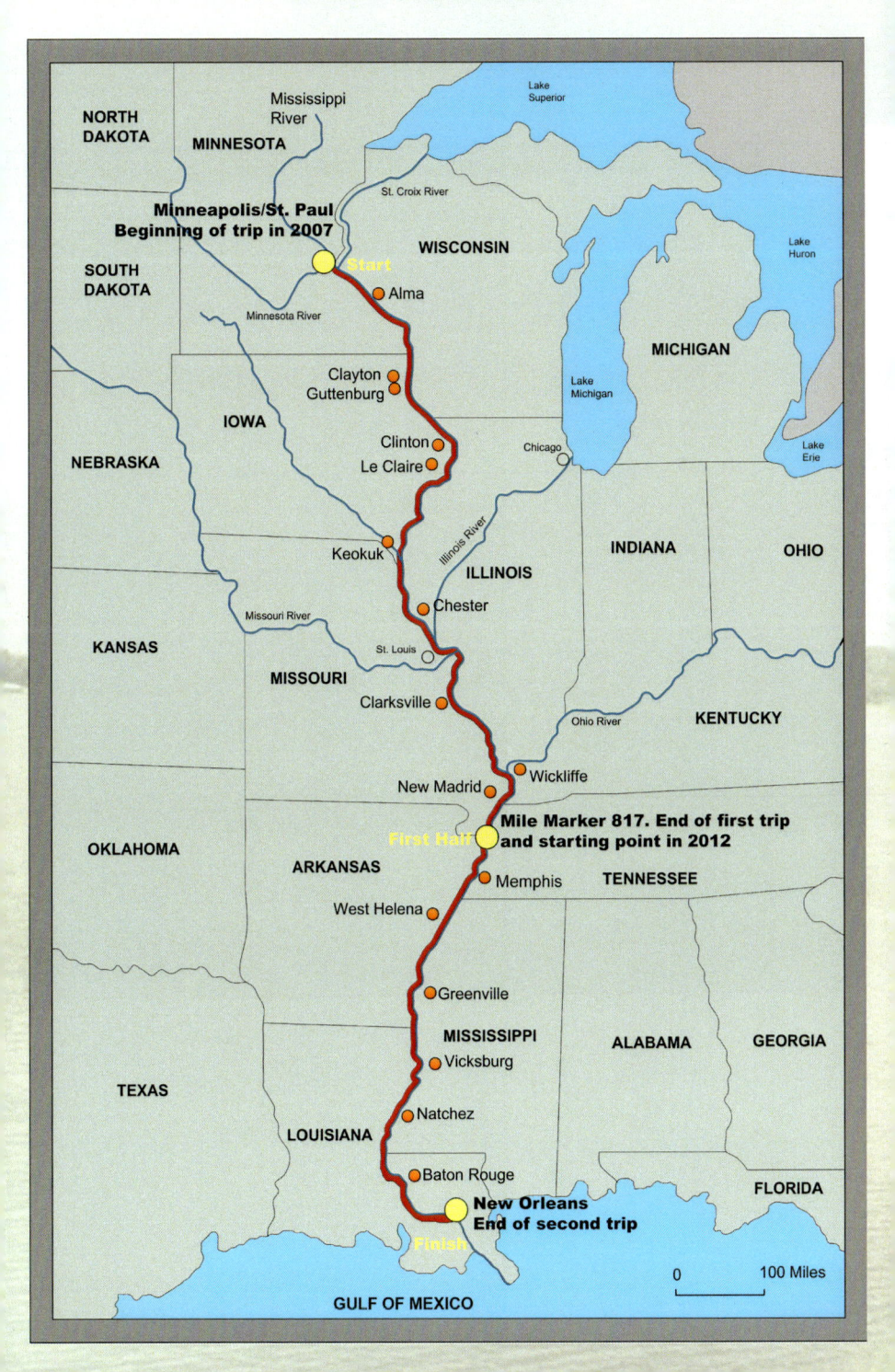

Foreword

"Such a long, long time to be gone and a short time to be there."
From "Box of Rain" by the Grateful Dead

I was not jumping for joy when my father asked if I would be interested in jet-skiing the Mississippi River from St. Paul, Minnesota, to New Orleans – an anticipated two-week, 1,700-mile journey.

That I'd be going with my older sister and parents was even less appealing. The four of us in the car for any length of time often resulted in loud disagreements and screaming matches.

Add to this that my father, whom I love dearly, had just started recuperating from a long, strenuous battle with non-Hodgkin lymphoma cancer, and the whole venture seemed a bit nuts.

The mere idea of it made my spine tingle with nervousness. But my dad's assurance, diligence and excitement sparked something inside of me.

I wanted to be part of this journey.

My sister Jennifer, too, was game. She was always up for adventures that included traveling at speeds of more than 60 miles per hour and spending time with Dad.

Our journey was indeed unpleasant at times because of arguments and disagreements. But it was also filled with laughter, fun and a closeness none of us had experienced together before.

We shared poems about fecal matter, swear words and the beautiful synchronicity a family experiences when overcoming some of life's most primal, life-threatening obstacles.

We uncovered personal mysteries deeper than the Mississippi; we addressed family feuds previously left untouched; and we struggled with the separation of mother and father and the constant temptation to accept defeat.

What kept us going were the precious moments in which we enjoyed the tenderness of new beginnings, friendships formed on frothy banks and fortune found in the strength of our reshaped family.

At the time, I had no idea the impact this journey would have on my life or that it would be one of the last great adventures with my sister.

It was on the banks of the Mississippi River that Jennifer and I finally rekindled our childhood bond, climbed over hurdles we didn't know possible and cried some and laughed much more.

It's where we became friends again. And our entire family took on a new shape and love.

I cannot thank my father enough for giving me the unbreakable gift and opportunity of a friendship with Jennifer.

Today, when I think of our journey down the Mississippi, I think of Jennifer, who, sadly, is no longer with us.

She passed on a quiet, snowy day in February 2016 at the terribly young age of 27, stolen from us by the unyielding grip and fury of drug addiction.

To say we are heartbroken doesn't capture our pain. We miss her every day.

Our journey down the Mississippi remains a cherished memory, and this story and the spirit she demonstrates in it is a tribute to her.

It is our hope that with this book we can create lasting conversation about drug addiction and assist others in their journey to sobriety.

For every copy sold, we will donate money to the Emerald Jenny Foundation, created in my sister's memory.

The foundation's mission is to help provide resources for families dealing with drug addiction.

For more information, please log onto one of our websites:
www.thebigmuddybook.com
www.emeraldjennyfoundation.org

Or, check out our Facebook page:
www.facebook.com/thebigmuddybook

Jackie Ayars

Chapter 1

Big Muddy, Here We Come

The idea for the trip down the Mississippi River came while poison dripped slowly into my arm.

I was 50 years old and recently diagnosed with non-Hodgkin lymphoma, a cancer of the lymphatic system that starts in white blood cells. Every third Friday for five months, I sat for eight hours at Fairview Hospital in Cleveland, undergoing chemotherapy treatments.

As cancers go, this wasn't the worst, according to my doctor.

"It's very aggressive, but it's very treatable," he told me.

"If you're gonna get cancer, this is what you should get."

I guess that should have made me feel better but it's hard to crack a smile when you've got a 3 ½-inch tumor growing inside your chest.

Toward the end of my chemotherapy in December 2006, I started thinking about taking an adventure. I wanted something to look forward to, something to celebrate my survival.

I still had a couple of months of radiation ahead, but I figured the toughest part was over.

During my long hours in chemotherapy, I read an article titled "One Hundred and One Days on the Mississippi" about how a guy named Guy Haglund canoed the Mississippi River in 101 days.

I liked the idea of an adventure down the Mississippi. It had a romantic feel to it, like a Mark Twain novel.

But I didn't want to travel in a canoe. I didn't have the time. I had two, maybe three, weeks of vacation to cover the 1,700 miles from St. Paul, Minnesota, to New Orleans.

So I thought about taking a motorcycle trip along the river. Motorcycles were fast, adventurous, fun.

Then I thought, "Too dangerous."

Hmmm.

What about jet skis? They're sort of like motorcycles on the water.

I had jet-skied a little before, so why not?

From that moment, I embraced the idea and never let go.

I liked the idea of a mission to accomplish, and I wanted

my family — wife, Nancy, and teenage daughters, Jennifer and Jackie — to be my team.

To my knowledge, no other women had jet-skied down the Mississippi.

My good friend and business partner, Larry Fischer, thought I was crazy.

"Are you out of your friggin' mind, taking your wife and kids on this trip?" he asked, noting they aren't the rugged outdoor types. "This is the ultimate guys trip."

But I wanted my family there.

Larry thought my goal was to pull the family together. Things had been rocky with Nancy and me for a while. And the girls? They fought constantly.

But I don't think that's why I wanted to do it. At least not consciously.

With my second chance at life, I wanted an adventure to show that I was still alive. And I wanted to nurture my relationship with my daughters. I had spent so much time working when they were younger. I wanted this opportunity to do something special with them.

I had no idea then how my journey conquering cancer and The Big Muddy would change my family and me, and bring me closer to my daughters along the way.

Sunday, July 22, 2007
Day 1: St. Paul, Minnesota, to Alma, Wisconsin

Jennifer and I were flying down the river having fun, each on our own jet ski. It was the first day of our trip and we were full of energy.

"I was pumped to be out doing something adventurous and to be experiencing something that no one I know had done," recalled Jennifer, who proudly wore her first pair of designer Armani sunglasses down the river.

She didn't want to wear the more practical sunglasses I had brought for her. Or use the band to keep them snug around her head.

She was too cool.

We left St. Paul, Minnesota, earlier that morning from beautiful Hidden Falls Regional Park, just below the first lock and dam on the river at mile marker 844.

Hidden Falls Park was one of the four original park areas selected for St. Paul in 1887 by noted landscape architect Horace Cleveland. Coincidentally, Cleveland was a descendant of Moses Cleaveland, who founded Cleveland, Ohio, in 1796.

Huge, towering cottonwood trees dotted the shoreline of the park and Jackie marveled at their massive, claw-like roots that arched out of the ground and into the water.

Our destination that day was Alma, Wisconsin, 95 miles away.

We dubbed Jackie "The Navigator" because she and Nancy stayed off the river and drove the Jeep. Their mission was to pick up Jennifer and me at each destination.

The pairings were intentional.

"If Jackie and I had to spend a day in the car together, we wouldn't have made it to the ramp," Jennifer said. "We would have been fighting and one of us would have been left behind."

Two Jet Skis: Stop!

About an hour into our trip, I looked in my rear view mirror and saw flashing red lights atop a boat manned by the Department of Natural Resources, which patrols the river.

"I wonder if we should pull over," I thought.

Soon, we heard a booming voice on a loudspeaker: "Two jet skis! Stop what you're doing immediately and turn off your engines!"

The boat pulled up next to us and an official asked for our identification and registration. He wanted to know why we had walkie-talkies.

I didn't tell him we were on a two-week journey, headed for New Orleans. We had just started our adventure and the destination didn't seem real yet.

Jennifer was quiet and nervous during the stop.

"I thought I was in trouble," she said. "I was on probation for DUI, but my dad didn't know that. I wasn't supposed to leave the state unless I told my probation officer. And I didn't."

Turns out our "offense" was simply riding too close together. They gave us a warning and off we went.

After that, things went smoothly for a while, even though it was slow going at times.

There were locks and dams about every 25 miles.

We often had to wait for long periods, sometimes hours, to be let through. We'd pass the time by studying our maps or just lying back on the jet skis and resting.

The 27 locks and dams on the Upper Mississippi, as we

learned, were built to control the water levels and tame a series of rapids on the Upper Mississippi from St. Paul to St. Louis, Missouri.

Over this 600-mile stretch, the water fell more than 400 feet, often through boulders, rapids or small waterfall systems.

The first lock and dam was built in 1913 near Keokuk, Iowa. Twenty years later, the U.S. Army Corps of Engineers started to build another lock and dam to control the rapids near Rock Island, Illinois.

Since then, 25 more have been added along the Upper Mississippi.

Entering a lock was sort of like getting into a full bathtub. Once inside, water poured out to lower you to the next portion of the river.

It's kind of like a series of steps that allows boats and barges to "walk" up and down the river.

A Romantic River Turns Treacherous

About halfway through our trip that day, a storm hit. The rain and wind stirred up the river something fierce.

"The waves were huge," Jennifer said. "They were washing over the front of my jet ski and into my face and over my head. I was soaked. And I was getting thrown around and beat up."

At one point, she stood up and a wave crashed into her, almost knocking her off her jet ski.

"I put my head down, and when I looked up, I saw my sunglasses float right off the back," Jennifer said. "I almost went after them.

"I turned the jet ski off and just sat there. I didn't care if I capsized. Then a big wave came and almost capsized me and I was like, OK, and I turned it back on and got going."

Jennifer screamed to get my attention but I couldn't hear her. My walkie-talkie was turned off.

"Dad! I don't know what to do!" she shouted.

When she finally caught up to me, she glared.

"What the hell?!" she said. "Where's your walkie-talkie? I could have died behind you. I could have died!"

It didn't get any better when we reached Lake Pepin at about 2 o'clock that day. The lake, the largest on the Mississippi, was about two miles wide. Traveling through it was wicked because we rode straight into a headwind and the waves really picked up.

"I'm looking left and I'm looking right, and I can't see shit," Jennifer said. "When we sped up, [the rain] felt like you were getting nailed in the face by rocks.

"And I had no sunglasses, so I couldn't keep my eyes open. My hair was like a bird's nest. Our rain gear did nothing. I was miserable."

We spent an hour battling the whitecaps. The air was cold and my hands started to get numb with the wind in my face and the waves crashing down on me.

No wonder, as I found during my research, experts say you need at least an 18-foot boat to withstand the waves and wakes on the river. Our jet skis were only 12 feet long.

But I thought if we could just get to the end of the lake,

things would get back to normal.

We arrived safely in Alma, but the girls' nerves were frayed. It didn't help that a woman we met that night warned us of whirlpools she claimed could pull entire boats under.

She was referring to the strong currents created by wing dams. But they do not "eat" boats.

The first wing dam was designed and built in 1879 under the leadership of Captain James B. Eads.

Eads was famous for building the country's first steel bridge, which still spans the Mississippi River and connects St. Louis, Missouri, to East St. Louis, Illinois.

His wing dam concept was even more significant.

Sediment build-up near the mouth of the Mississippi in New Orleans created sandbars that grounded the huge cargo ships critical to the port.

To alleviate the sediment buildup, Eads designed jetties, underwater walls running perpendicular to the shoreline. He was so confident the jetties would work, he told the government not to pay him unless he succeeded.

He did succeed, and now wing dams are used throughout the river.

Jackie didn't know this history and listened to that woman the first night.

"That lady really scared me," she said.

This wasn't the kind of start I had anticipated. I knew then that our trip was going to be more unpredictable and, perhaps, more dangerous than I had expected.

Chapter 2

"You Don't Know How Close to Death You Were"

My cancer journey — which led to my Mississippi River journey — began in July 2006.

I had a lingering cold and finally figured I should get it checked out.

So on July 7, I went to see my family doctor, Dr. John Wirtz.

I had lost 20 pounds quickly and without trying. That was a red flag, he said.

He ordered a chest X-ray.

I returned about a week later to learn the results.

"See that?" he said, pointing to a black spot near my lungs. "That's not supposed to be there."

He immediately sent me to see a thoracic surgeon, whom I coincidentally knew because my architectural firm was designing his medical office. He ordered a biopsy.

The results confirmed what Dr. Wirtz suspected: cancer.

My wife, Nancy, and I drove home to Bay Village that day and met Jennifer at the house.

I don't remember that day and neither does Nancy. Maybe I was in shock. Maybe denial.

But Jennifer, then 19, remembers it clearly.

She thought it was odd that I was home in the middle of the day because I was always at the office.

"He said, 'Hey, we need to talk to you,' in kind of one of those tones and had that look that I had never seen before," Jennifer recalled.

"At first, I was in disbelief and then I don't even know. I don't even know what happened after they told me.

"Something broke inside."

The Complications

After my diagnosis, I didn't research my cancer on the Internet. I didn't look into the disease. I don't think I ever got down in the dumps about why it was happening to me.

I think it was harder on my family emotionally than on me. I'm not quite sure how to explain it, but there's something different about being a patient than watching someone close to you go through an illness.

Years earlier, a friend of mine was near death before he got a liver transplant. I visited him a couple of days before the transplant, and he looked awful.

I went home that day and immediately took Jackie and Jennifer to get the dog they had been begging for.

My wife didn't approve but I thought: "Life's too short. Why not?"

With my cancer, I didn't have that knee-jerk reaction.

The severity didn't hit me until a conversation with my doctor on my last day of chemotherapy.

Still, it was a harrowing experience, especially when I ran into complications.

One day, between my diagnosis and the start of my chemotherapy, I passed out in the basement. My wife found me near the dehumidifier that I was trying to empty. She drove me to the hospital.

I sat in an exam room when a staff member walked in and told me I needed blood thinners. To administer them, I'd have to give myself a shot each day.

I told him I couldn't do that. I hated needles.

He told me I couldn't leave the hospital until he saw me do it.

I wanted to leave so badly, so I took the needle, lifted up my shirt, pricked my belly and squeezed the medicine in.

Then I hurried out the door and down the hallway to the car, where Nancy was waiting. When I sat down in the passenger seat, I realized my shirt was untucked and buttoned crookedly.

Sometimes, at home, my hand shook so badly that I couldn't give myself the shot. I had to ask Nancy to do it. But my pride eventually steadied my hand and I did it myself.

As uncomfortable as that was, it wasn't the worst of my complications.

Before chemo began, doctors surgically inserted a port into my chest. That's where the poison would be administered to try to rid my body of the cancer.

I didn't feel good when I got home after the surgery. So I went to lie down. Nancy came into the bedroom to check on me and took one look at my swollen, purplish-blue face and said:

"Oh my God, Bill, you don't look good. You better go back to the hospital."

Doctors took a CT scan of my head. Then I waited. And waited. And waited, until I finally fell asleep.

I was jolted awake about 6 a.m. when Dr. Kevin Kerwin flung open the door to my room and rushed in.

Someone had finally read my scan and it showed a massive blood clot in the jugular vein in my neck. There was another clot in my arm.

They whisked me away to a room where the doctors cleared the clot and removed the port in my chest, which they suspected was causing the problems.

I think they put a balloon in my neck to open up the blockage. It felt so weird, as if everything stopped for a moment.

After that, I needed a blood transfusion.

After the blood transfusion, I started chemo.

It was a long, awful day.

I didn't know whether to laugh at my business partner Larry Fischer or throttle him when, in the midst of it all, he came in and said, "There's a proposal that's due tomorrow. Can we go over this?"

I think he was trying to distract me, but then again, he's not the warm-and-fuzzy type.

He did try to lighten the mood, though, by cracking a joke. He said if I got Tiger Woods' blood in the transfusion, it might improve my golf game.

Good old Larry.

Meanwhile, my daughters were feeling overwhelmed by my illness. Nancy called both of them to let them know I was in the hospital after my collapse.

Jennifer was at a bar and got drunk and never came home that night.

Jackie, 16, was at a friend's house. Because of the stress of the news, or something else, she fainted into our front door when she arrived home about midnight.

Nancy found her in a heap on the front porch and slept with her that night so she could keep an eye on her. She feared Jackie had a concussion.

The Treatments

One of the worst parts about the chemo was the repeated needle pricks. Because doctors removed the port from my chest, they administered the chemo drugs in my arm. And the constant pricking sucked.

I hate needles.

What's worse, I only had one "good" vein to administer the poison. I was at their mercy to find it and get it right.

My appointments started at 8 a.m. and ended at 4 p.m. In the beginning, my wife drove me, stayed awhile and later picked me up because I wasn't supposed to drive. But after a while, I just started driving myself and going through the treatments alone.

I didn't encourage visitors, especially my daughters. It wasn't so much that I wanted to protect them from my illness; I was just trying to keep things as normal as possible.

My parents, who were still in my hometown of Vermilion, Ohio, were older and couldn't travel to see me. Nancy, who worked at my firm, had to go to the office.

"I carried things on," she said.

I don't remember much about how I passed the time during my long treatments. I know I watched TV and read architectural magazines sometimes. And I'd talk to other patients and their families.

It was weird: There was one guy who had been in the hospital with me. He died while I was undergoing treatments.

There was another woman, a professional acquaintance, whose husband was getting chemo. He died, too.

I didn't fear death. At each appointment, I had tests and scans to determine if and how much the tumor was shrinking. The tests consistently showed it was. That reassured me.

Nancy wasn't scared and that helped, too.

"Neither one of us was all that worried," she said. "He just took at it as a challenge and thought, 'I just have to do what the doctors tell me.'"

After each chemo treatment, I was on a high for several days. On Monday, I'd go in for a shot to get my blood cell count up.

One day I sat next to a fellow patient and she said, "Do you know how much that shot costs? Ten-thousand dollars!"

I had no idea.

After the shot, I'd go through a low where I didn't have much energy. Still, I'd go to work.

"He would always go to the office when he shouldn't have," Jackie said. "He's very old school with the man role, taking care of the family and being strong. And he tried to keep that up when he was sick."

A Warm Coat is A Small Comfort

After I told my partners about my cancer, I thought about how we had decided to name our firm Perspectus Architecture, instead of putting our own names on the door. We made the decision because we wanted the firm to continue long after we were gone. I just didn't think I'd be the first one at risk to go.

Even though Jennifer and Jackie were still living at home, I didn't see them much during my treatments.

My cancer terrified them.

Jennifer disappeared into work at the Saucy Bistro in Westlake. When she wasn't working long hours, she'd drink and self-medicate with drugs.

Jackie bolted town and spent a lot of time in Dayton, visiting a boyfriend and "couch-surfing" from house to house. When she was home, she came to the hospital occasionally.

She remembers one visit vividly.

"He was lying in bed and he couldn't really talk and he was puking," Jackie said. "It was the first time I had ever even seen him sick. That was the first time I saw him as a person.

"I always thought my parents were invincible. It put him in this light that he was a fragile person. That he wasn't always this strong rock. It was definitely an awakening. It was terrifying."

The dramatic change in my looks scared my daughters, too.

"He was just white and didn't have any eyebrows or hair," Jackie said.

Losing my hair wasn't that big of a deal, but when I lost my eyelashes and eyebrows? That's when I started to look weird.

And if chemo wasn't bad enough, I contracted shingles during my treatment. The viral infection caused an excruciatingly painful rash.

In my wildest imagination, I never realized how awful it could be.

It was so unbearable that the doctors prescribed the powerful painkiller oxycodone. That drug scared the shit out of me because it made me feel so good. My head felt clear, my body pain-free.

I can see how people get addicted to it.

I took it twice a day for a while but didn't renew my prescription.

My other side effects weren't as bad as shingles, thankfully.

I got really cold a lot, especially during the winter. Jackie took me shopping for a warm coat. I never go clothes shopping. I don't like it.

But she insisted.

We went to the mall and looked around for what seemed like forever. Jackie wanted to find a pea coat with a hood. But turns out they don't make pea coats with hoods. At least we couldn't find any.

We finally settled on a nice, hoodless pea coat with matching hat and gloves. I would have never bought it on my own, but Jackie insisted.

In December, I finished my treatment. It was a monumental relief to be done and to look ahead.

It was at this milestone that the idea for the river trip began to take root.

Betcha A Dollar I'll Do It

The planning for the trip didn't really happen until two things occurred:

First, my doctor told me I was lucky to be alive.

Second, I made a dollar bet with my friend Mike Liezert.

On my final day of chemotherapy, Dr. Kevin Kerwin — the doctor who took charge when my blood clots were discovered — checked up on me.

He didn't recognize me at first and asked why we hadn't met in the past six months. I told him we had — on the morning he discovered my blood clots.

"Holy shit! You don't know how close to death you were," he told me. "People don't get that close to death and survive. If you were a little older or sick, there was no way."

Wow. I knew that had been a tough patch, but it never dawned on me that I had almost died.

I went home and immediately began to create a bucket list.

"There's all kinds of shit I want to do," I thought.

I don't remember what I wrote down, other than to join Westwood Country Club.

That's probably because soon after I started my list, my wife told me I was crazy. I thought she was worried about how much it would cost.

Nancy says it wasn't about the money.

"His bucket list was about him. It wasn't about everybody," she said. "When you're married, it's just not about one person."

But she had become very concerned about money after I got sick. We still had a lot of debt from starting the architectural firm years ago. I had emptied my 401K to help start Perspectus — just before September 11, 2001, and the World Trade Center attacks.

It wasn't a good time financially.

Now, Nancy wanted us to pay off our debt and get on firmer financial footing. She tried to push to make sure I didn't wallow in any sorrow. I think that was a good thing.

"I'm just not a pessimistic person," she said. "You go on, that's all."

So, I crumpled up my bucket list into a ball and threw it away.

I held onto the idea for the Mississippi River trip, though. And at an out-of-town conference soon after, I made a bet with my buddy Mike that I'd do it.

We had a tradition of making $1 bets. And although the stakes were small, no one wanted to lose.

The Buy In

Part of the excitement for the trip was looking forward to spending time with my daughters, who, as teenagers, were starting to go their separate ways.

My wife had pretty much raised Jennifer and Jackie because I worked so much, often spending late nights and weekends at the office. Later, I went back to school to get my MBA, which took me away even more.

"When I was younger, he wasn't really around a lot," Jennifer says. "My most prominent memories of my dad are at the dinner table. They're not him going to softball games or my tae kwon do practices. It was the dinner table. The majority of the dinner table conversations were about work.

"As a kid, I just thought that was the way it was. I didn't know any other way … He was just a busy guy making a career and life for himself."

I wanted this trip to be a bonding time with my girls. Though we had taken family vacations before, the Mississippi trip was going to be my biggest undertaking with them: Two weeks, 1,700 miles on the river. I'd need them every step of the way.

I asked Jennifer first, figuring she'd be the most enthusiastic since she was the most adventurous of the three.

We were upstairs in my second-floor office one day when I casually asked: "Hey, would you like to jet-ski the Mississippi River with me?"

"I thought my dad might be losing his mind after all the chemo," Jennifer recalled. "It was definitely over the top, definitely crazy. That's what made it so awesome."

She was in.

"I hadn't been there when he was going through all his cancer, so I felt like this was something I could do for him," she said. "It was the triumph of overcoming. I wanted to be a part of that."

Persuading Jackie and my wife proved more challenging.

Jackie was scared of jet-skiing and the Mississippi River. When she was 8, I took her jet-skiing in Florida and it terrified her. Now so, too, did the thought of navigating a large river with alligators and other dangers.

But she agreed to do it because, like Jennifer, she knew it was important to me.

Plus I made a big deal about how great a feat it would be

for us to accomplish.

My wife, however, was not excited.

"I just remember thinking, 'Can't you go on the trip with the guys?'" she said. "'Why do I have to go? Why do our kids have to go?'

"I didn't want to go. But he doesn't take no for an answer."

So she jumped on board.

Well, sort of.

Chapter 3

The Seaweed Debacle

Most families go to the beach on vacation.

Here I was, on a sometimes fierce, lonely river, jet-skiing with mine.

But I was on a mission.

I had 10 books for 10 days.

Each notebook-size, laminated book contained maps of the river and showed the mile markers and boat ramps along the way.

On the front of each, I put the start and finish points that

I expected to follow each day.

I carried the day's map with me on the jet ski.

Each morning, before we backed the skis into the river, I got up early to locate a ramp near our destination. I also pinpointed possible gas stops along the way.

My challenge was to correctly calculate the distance from our starting point to our exit ramp so we wouldn't run out of fuel.

We rode on two blue and white Sea-Doo GTX, 155 horsepower "luxury" jet skis because they used regular gas instead of premium. They could reach a top speed of about 60 mph and boasted better gas mileage than the 215 horsepower models.

But I quickly learned "better" gas mileage was relative.

During my planning, I figured we could go 200-300 miles on the 16-gallon gas tank.

But in reality, it turned out we only got 5 miles to the gallon because we traveled at top speed most of the time. That meant we could go 80 miles max before we had to stop or refuel.

On the first leg up North, that wasn't a problem. There were lots of marinas along the way, so we could fill up whenever we needed.

But as we got farther south, it became remote.

"I felt like Christopher Columbus," Jennifer said.

The Seaweed Debacle

Once we got started, I realized our journey was so much more than a leisurely trip down a romantic river.

And I quickly learned that planning is not execution.

Despite my six months of detailed preparation with maps, lists and mathematical calculations, we faced lots of surprises and snafus along the way.

On Day 1, I lost my map. Sunk right to the bottom of the river.

I also discovered I couldn't use my headphones for my walkie-talkie because they kept blowing off. (We didn't have iPhones then.)

So when Jennifer was amusing herself by shouting, "It's a negative tango, over and out!" into her walkie talkie, I couldn't hear her.

"Why isn't this guy answering me?" she wondered. "I'm funny! Laugh!"

But the biggest debacle early on was our messy encounter with seaweed.

We were in Clinton, Iowa, near mile marker 523. We had covered more than 300 miles so far on our trip and about 80 miles that day.

Jennifer and I rode the jet skis for the third straight day. Jackie and Nancy drove the Jeep.

It was 4 o'clock and we had been on the river for about five hours.

It was friggin' hot and humid, with temps in the mid-90s. The sun hung low, creating bright reflections on the water, making it hard to see where we were going.

We reached a lock and dam and cut our engines.

Time to wait.

We studied the map to find a ramp nearby. We found one about a mile or two away at a local campground.

I sent a locator pin from my cell phone to the laptop in the Jeep, so Jackie and Nancy could find us.

It was pretty cool that I could use Garmin GPS technology to pinpoint ramp locations and share them electronically.

Jackie became so reliant on her laptop during our trip, she gave it a name: Garmina. Nancy and Jennifer called it Laptop Lady.

My Indiana Jones Moment

I didn't want to wait to get through the lock that day. I was tired and it was getting close to dusk and harder to see.

So, I decided to zip straight across the river toward the ramp at the campground.

(I was unaware at the time that there was a boating channel and it was important to stay in it.)

Jennifer followed me but yelled: "I don't think this is a good idea!"

I kept going.

Soon, our engines started to falter.

"I could tell it didn't have the 'oomph' that it always had," Jennifer said.

"Dad, don't do this!" she pleaded.

"No, it's going to be fine," I said. "Just gun it and it will be fine."

But our engines continued to weaken. Jennifer finally stopped.

I kept going.

I soon realized there were lily pads or some type of seaweed just under the surface of the water that were clogging our engines.

I slowed down and glanced back. I saw smoke coming from the jet ski's exhaust.

I cut the engine.

Shit.

I was stuck.

Jennifer sped toward me and then killed her engine, so her jet ski wouldn't clog further.

She grabbed her wooden paddle and paddled to me. We tied together and sat.

Beauty and Tears To the Rescue

We knew the ramp was near. But it was around a bend, so we couldn't see it or signal to Jackie and Nancy.

I started to worry.

We were too far to swim to shore.

We couldn't restart our engines.

And I didn't know how long we could paddle our jet skis through the thick, seaweed-filled water.

We called Jackie and Nancy.

Jackie was scared and anxious. She started to cry.

How would we reach the ramp?

In one of the many coincidences — or perhaps just lucky moments — during our trip, there was an airboat at the campground.

Airboats are designed to navigate easily through swampy, mucky water.

In tears, Jackie, persuaded the guys from the Department of Natural Resources to go out in their airboat and tow us in.

The airboat pulled us out of the seaweed and toward the ramp. But before we reached land, I needed to try to unclog the jet skis.

"So Indiana Jones dives into the river," Jennifer said.

She remembers me cutting the seed weed out with a knife. I remember pulling it out with my hands.

Either way, I was in the mucky, uncertain waters trying desperately to save our jet skis and our trip.

"That was terrifying," Jennifer said. "I thought, 'He's going to get eaten by a water serpent or alligator!'"

But during this experience on the river — and the many other stressful ones we shared — Jennifer started to understand working as a team with me.

"For the first time, we treated each other with a mutual respect that we never had," she said. "He was always the father and I was the daughter.

"It was different for my dad to rely on me on the river."

One By One, Melting Down

We all knew the physical challenge was to reach New Orleans. But once on our journey, there was an emotional challenge, too.

"We were just trying to make it together," Jennifer said.

But it was tough to keep Jennifer and Jackie motivated,

focused and getting along.

"That was our personal hell," Jennifer said of being on the trip with her sister.

Nancy didn't help things.

The girls took their cues from her, so when "she wasn't into it, I wasn't into it," Jackie said.

As a result, there were multiple meltdowns.

First, Jennifer flipped out that first day when she lost her Armani sunglasses. It was like the whole world had turned to shit.

The next day, Jackie said, "I'm going home. Get me a bus ticket."

Then, on Day 5 outside of St. Louis, Nancy told me she wanted to end the trip.

"A lot of it had to do with the kids," she said. "Jennifer and Jackie really never got along... One would want to do something, the other wouldn't. Our family dynamics...so many strong-willed people. We just didn't really get along.

"It just culminated at that point. I wanted to just kill Bill. I didn't want to be there. I was just done. I didn't want to be with him anymore. He was just super-selfish."

I was furious she wanted to quit. I blew up.

"My dad does not yell a lot at all. … but when he does, it is scary and it does not make me feel good," Jennifer said.

Nancy didn't care that I wanted to finish the trip.

"My mom was not being a team player," Jennifer said. "And I think that was huge for everyone … I remember my dad saying, 'If we can't make this work out here, then there's no point in us working on it back home.'"

I vaguely remember saying that, but much of that night is fuzzy because I was so angry.

I went to a bar after Nancy and I fought. She went back to the hotel with the girls.

I found out later that while they were flipping through the TV channels, Jackie said, 'You know, I think we should all smoke a doob."

Nancy agreed.

The girls were thrilled that their mom wanted to smoke a joint with them for the first time.

"You're the Only One"

As I sat stewing, alone in the bar, I thought, 'This is ridiculous. We have to figure this out and come to some sort of agreement.'"

I wanted to finish the trip.

I thought it was typical of Nancy to change her mind midstream and think, "What's the big deal about doing this trip?"

It was a reflection on the rest of our relationship. She's willing to change direction, and I want to stick with the commitment.

"I was more fickle, and he's very routine-oriented," Nancy said.

But I share some of the blame for Nancy's meltdown and desire to quit. I was wacked out because we were off schedule.

I had 10 books, 10 days. That was the mission.

I ignored everything else.

The girls weren't surprised that Nancy and I were at odds. They had seen it before.

"I just thought that's how they are on vacation," Jackie said. "I felt like my dad was being really selfish.

"But really, in the end, I was the one being selfish. I just thought the whole trip was really dangerous. It was a really big internal struggle for me. I wanted to do it for my dad, but not if it's going to kill us.

"I thought, 'You survived this horrible cancer and now you want to kill all of us?' I should have had a little bit more faith."

I didn't realize then — or maybe I just didn't listen to — how scared Jackie was of the river.

I blew off her worries.

I didn't engage with her and Jennifer, as I should have. I needed them. I should have realized that somehow there's got to be a way to make it a little less emotional. Maybe I could have created things for them to look forward to.

But I wasn't prepared for how badly the trip would go. I never thought we wouldn't get along. I never thought we'd have trouble focusing on task.

"You're the only one," Jennifer told me. "Mom was not made to ever go on that trip. It was terrible."

"You Have a Death Wish"

The next morning, the drinks and marijuana had helped cool tempers, and, without discussion, we continued on.

But morale was definitely at a low point.

So I decided to alter our route. We skipped the next 162 miles on the river and drove to Chester, Illinois (mile marker 112), which was southeast of St. Louis.

Along the way we passed through Cape Girardeau, Missouri, the birthplace of conservative talk-show host Rush Limbaugh.

When we reached Chester, we put the jet skis back in the water and kept going.

I guess that's kind of "cheating" but I thought we could come back and cover this stretch another time.

I felt it was more important to keep going without long interruptions, since our team was so fragile.

The next day was uneventful and we made it the next 112 miles on the river in peace.

On Day 7, we headed to Tennessee.

The morning started out sunny and bright but when we got on the river that afternoon, clouds rolled in. We saw the rain coming but it looked like a narrow band that would pass quickly.

Jennifer said, "Let's go!" And off we went into the rain.

The water pelted our face and felt like needles on our skin.

We finally stopped under a bridge and waited until the rain passed. I saw more clouds in the distance, but it looked like they were moving west to east. I figured we could stay ahead of the storm if we rode 60 mph south.

What I forgot is that the river meanders back and forth. So when we rounded a bend, the compass showed us heading northwest, straight into the storm.

And this time, it wasn't just rain. Thunder roared and fierce lightning lit up the sky.

I looked into my rearview mirror to check on Jennifer. She had stopped.

I turned around and pulled alongside of her.

"I'm done," she said. "You have a death wish."

The look in her eye made it very clear that she meant it.

The situation made me think of the movie "Forrest Gump," when, in the midst of a fierce ocean storm, Lieutenant Dan says: "You call this a storm?"

But I didn't dare joke with Jennifer now.

Fortunately, we had just passed a ramp, so we turned around, anchored the jet skis in the sand and walked up the ramp to look for cover.

I sent our location to Jackie and Nancy in the Jeep. We were about 80 miles north of Memphis — and 700 miles from New Orleans.

We put on our raincoats and it was the worst friggin' rain gear. The shit absorbed water.

Jennifer was drenched. She took off the rain gear and threw it down.

A couple sitting in a truck nearby waved us over and asked us if we wanted to wait out the storm with them.

Another stroke of luck.

What the heck were they doing here, in the middle of nowhere, on a stormy day? We never found out, but we talked and laughed with Doug and Sandra until the storm ended. The sun came out and it was almost as if it never happened.

Nancy and Jackie were on the other side of the river when we sent them our location, so it took them about an hour to pick us up.

With Jackie at the wheel, the Jeep came flying down the dirt road, dust kicking up everywhere and the jet-ski trailer bouncing up and down.

Doug and Sandra couldn't believe they found us.

We loaded the jet skis on the trailer, jumped in the Jeep and headed to the hotel in Memphis for the night.

"We just weren't ready to be built"

Without Jennifer on board, I feared our adventure was really over this time.

Despite her meltdown, Jennifer was my biggest advocate and faithful co-pilot.

Jackie and Nancy had no interest in riding a jet ski.

They told me: If you want to continue, we'll drop you in the river and you can have at it. But we're going home.

I went down to the marina to figure out how to get to the next ramp. I was pissed. Nothing was working.

I had spent six months planning this trip.

I had 10 maps for 10 days.

I had a mission!

But it was clear that the family needed a rest. So, we spent a day in Memphis sightseeing. I hoped the break from the river might rejuvenate Nancy and the girls to continue.

But things remained tense.

Jackie got sick from a nasty migraine. At Graceland, she

refused to go inside with us and took off while we were touring the mansion. We found her later walking around Memphis.

"I'm going home," she said.

I knew then that our adventure was truly over.

We drove north to Land Between the Lakes National Recreation Area, where we relaxed, swam and went rafting for a few days.

It helped everyone recover.

I tried to console myself. We had made it nearly 1,000 miles. We raised about $4,000 for the Fairview Hospital Community West Foundation, the hospital that cared for me during my cancer.

We did pretty well, right?

But as we drove home, I felt disappointed. Our team had fallen apart. We aborted the mission. The family bond I wanted to build never developed.

"We just weren't ready to be built," Jackie said.

Chapter 4

Phoenix

She said she was going out with a girlfriend. I didn't think anything of it.

Until she didn't come back.

It was December 2009. The week before Christmas. We were planning the company holiday party at our house.

Things had improved for Nancy and me the past two years, since our fight on The Big Muddy.

We were talking more and arguing less.

"Things were better…" Nancy said.

But on Friday, December 18, she went out with a girlfriend. She went out again on Saturday — and never came home.

The next morning she sent me a text. I don't remember the details of the message. All I remember is that suddenly, everything got weird.

She showed up Monday morning at the office.

Did she really stay at her friend's house? I asked.

No, she said. She was with a guy. And she planned to stay with him.

In the next breath, she said, "I'll still help with the Christmas party."

Are you fucking kidding me?! I said. Then I fired her.

Typical Nancy fashion: She acted like it was no big deal.

Wild from the Start

Weird. That's the word I use over and over to describe what happened, although I know I have many other less printable feelings.

One of the hardest things to accept about our breakup was that despite a number of ups and downs over the years, we really seemed to be getting along well the past couple of years.

For her to leave then — and so quickly — baffled me. I didn't understand how she could leave me for someone she had met just a few days earlier.

"I felt like there was always something missing when I was married to Bill," Nancy said. "We were so opposite …

"When I met Michael, we just clicked and something got

going," she said. "I didn't really cheat on Bill. I just left him."

Nancy and I met at my first job, when we worked together at Collins, Rimer and Gordon Architects in Cleveland. I was an architect. She was a secretary.

Her sister and a friend of mine set us up on our first date. From the beginning, it was crazy and intense.

One of my most vivid early memories of us is in my Corvette. The top was down and the sun was shining. I looked over and she had pulled her top down. Off we sped. It was a wild ride!

My friends thought it would never last because we were too different. I didn't care; we were having an awesome time.

Nancy was so impetuous and fun. I loved that.

We dated for about a year before we married.

"I wanted someone who was a good provider and I wanted kids," Nancy said. "At that time in my life, he was the perfect person for me."

I wanted a family, too, and Jennifer and Jackie were born soon after Nancy and I married.

But then things got rocky. Really rocky.

"I wasn't always faithful to Bill," Nancy said.

She had an affair after Jackie was born. She took the kids and left. Initially, I was clueless about where they went or why she left.

I found her living with another man.

It was an awful experience. On top of the stress of her leaving, the kids were young, we had very little money and work was really demanding.

I moved forward with a divorce. It was nearly complete when we decided to reconcile.

I was pro-marriage; I wanted to patch things up. We went through counseling.

This was a defining moment. I felt strongly that we should stay together as a family. But as I look back, I don't think I ever recommitted 100 percent to the marriage after that.

A Traditional Marriage

Nancy stayed at home to raise the kids while I worked long hours at the firm. She didn't like me staying at the office late.

"I hated it," she said. "I only wanted him to be home for dinner… so we could sit down as a family. He would say that he would be home and then he wouldn't be home on time. I was home alone a lot by myself with the kids."

My time away increased when I went back to school in 1999 to get my MBA and later, in 2001, when Larry Fischer and I set off to start our own firm.

We had a one-year, no-compete clause with our former firm, so we started quietly.

Financially, it was a strain. I emptied my 401K and borrowed my dad's pickup truck for a while because I had to return my former firm's company car.

After three months, Nancy asked, "How long are you going to try this?"

I said, "There is no going back. This is not a trial run."

My focus on work and building my new firm created a lot of resentment with Nancy.

"He was just about himself when we were married," she said. "He didn't care about what I wanted to do. I wanted to open up a smoothie shop; he didn't care. I wanted to buy houses and rent them; he didn't care.

"It wasn't going to happen because it wasn't his dream."

It wasn't so much that I didn't support her, but I wondered about her commitment to her ideas. Often, Nancy would have an idea, run with it 100 percent — until she got another idea. So I questioned whether she had the motivation to see a business through. I wasn't willing to invest on a whim.

Missing Pieces

Our different parenting styles created tension, too.

Nancy said I sat back and watched things happen with our girls. She wanted me to be a more heavy-handed, imposing dad.

"I was the one who had to be the bad guy," she said. "What I needed from him was to be a strong father and for the kids to fear him…"

But that's not my style. I prefer to understand why someone thinks or acts a certain way, not scold them for it.

"Even if he knows I'm wrong, he's open to seeing how and why I've come to that conclusion," Jennifer said. "So it can help him understand me as a person."

Throughout our marriage, Nancy and I struggled to understand each other and our different styles.

"That connectedness was missing," she said.

No Going Back

When I found out Nancy was leaving me, I didn't attempt to repair things or ask her to come back.

This was her second affair. We were done. Period.

"He never called me and said, 'Nancy, you really upset me. I feel betrayed.' He never once called and said, 'Wow, I miss you.'

"I didn't want him to do that, but I expected something."

I don't know how she could expect that. She left, without a word. There was no fight, no "I'm leaving."

I didn't have anything left to invest in a reconciliation.

My focus was on protecting the kids and my assets. I assumed her having an affair would play in my favor. But it didn't matter in court.

Fortunately, custody wasn't an issue. Jennifer was 22, and Jackie was 20.

I tried to look at the divorce as a business transaction, mainly to keep myself sane.

I sold the new Miata with leather seats that I had just bought for her and bought a Jeep for myself instead.

The divorce proceedings went quickly.

By March 2010, we were no longer husband and wife.

Healing With My Daughters

I spent hours in therapy, focused on getting through the divorce and understanding my new relationship with my kids.

Then one day, I asked Nancy why she left.

She gave me a list of reasons: I was inflexible and stubborn. I didn't help around the house.

I don't remember the rest.

I really try to put things in boxes as best I can. Life can be so overwhelming.

So like my cancer, I don't talk about my divorce much.

In many ways, it was worse than cancer: more hurtful, more mysterious, more damaging to my family.

The girls, especially Jackie, took it hard.

"I was always a mama's girl," Jackie said. "My dad wasn't around a lot ... so from an early age, I just clung onto my mom. I just always thought if they were arguing, my mom just looked like the golden girl all my life.

"Then when they got divorced, I thought, 'Holy shit! My mom's totally not perfect!' It was an awakening. Maybe my mom was doing things wrong also in the relationship.

"I was really mad at her for a long time. For a couple years, I didn't really talk to her."

After Nancy left, I took the girls for a family picture. I wanted to document our new family.

Together, we began to heal and grow closer.

"My dad and I really formed a strong, real bond right after my mom left," Jennifer said.

Jackie and I built our relationship, too.

"At night, we'd have a couple of beers together and talk about everything and that really helped us bond," Jackie said. "We'd just talk a lot, more than we ever had.

"Sometimes I get sad because we're never going to sit down and go out to dinner, all of us together as a family, my mom, dad, Jennifer and I.

"But that divorce was totally for the best for everyone."

Nancy now lives in Phoenix, Arizona, with her boyfriend. That's why I nicknamed her Phoenix.

We keep in touch because of the girls. Our relationship is civil.

"Bill is a good guy: honest, hardworking," Nancy said. "I don't wish him any bad luck."

It was a wild ride.

Jennifer, left, and Jackie get ready to take on The Big Muddy as we leave home in Bay Village, Ohio. Both were teenagers in 2007.

The First Leg of Our Journey
ST. PAUL TO MEMPHIS

July 2007

The girls get the jet skis ready for the first day of our journey.

Jennifer will ride with me.

The Mississippi River through Minneapolis-St. Paul was amazingly beautiful.

Jackie was so young but did well driving the Jeep and finding us.

Jennifer leads the way through a lock and dam, a kind of elevator system on the river.

ABOVE: Drying out the gear after the first day.
LEFT: Jennifer and I arrive in Alma, Wisconsin, happy to be off the river at the end of the first day.

The tugs and barges were so enormous on the river. We stayed clear of them.

Jackie became so reliant on her laptop, she called it "Garmina," after the Garmin technology we used to find each other.

Jennifer waits on the river.

A glimpse of Jennifer and me on the river. The river was a half-mile wide or more in some places.

ABOVE/RIGHT: Jackie enjoyed sightseeing during the trip.

Jennifer enjoying some time off the river.

This park in Winona, Minnesota, sat right on the river.

On Day 3 of our trip, in Clinton, Iowa, an airboat had to tow our stalled jet skis out of thick seaweed.

I finally get Jackie to ride.

After the only day Jackie rode with me on the river, she was whipped. We were glad to be on land that night.

This couple, Doug and Sandra, let us sit in their truck during a downpour on the final day of our 2007 trip.

The jet skis are ready for another journey.

Jackie and Susan enjoying lunch on the way to Memphis, Tennessee.

The Second Leg of Our Journey
MEMPHIS TO NEW ORLEANS

August 2012

Jackie, Susan and I leave Cincinnati on our way to Memphis to start the second half of our Mississippi River trip. Jennifer will meet us there. It has been five years since Jackie, Jennifer, their mom and I ended our first trip down The Big Muddy. We never reached our final destination, New Orleans.

Day 1 started 80 miles north of Memphis, at the same spot where we ended our first trip. Here Jennifer, Jackie and I are revved up to continue our journey.

Unlike the first trip, both Jackie and Jennifer were excited to take on The Big Muddy this time.

Jennifer and I ride the jet skis together again as we leave our launch spot in Memphis.

We were exhausted when we arrived in West Helena, Arkansas, on Day 2. Jennifer was sunburned and the 91-degree heat wore us down.

Jackie enjoyed learning about the history of the south during our trip. Here, she explores the famous Blues Trail on Highway 61, named after the famous blues artists who traveled along it.

Jackie plays in the "Mississippi Mud" as she waits for Jennifer and me to arrive on Day 2 in West Helena, Arkansas.

A few drinks always helped us relax, but, no, Jackie did not drink all of these herself.

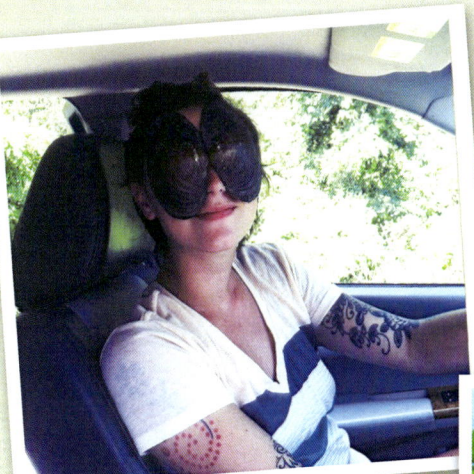

Jackie got creative when she had to wait for us to arrive. Here, she models clamshells.

This ramp in Greenville, Mississippi, was too unstable for us to use.

We stayed at The Greenville Inn in Mississippi on the second night. It was one of several historic accommodations we enjoyed on the trip.

On Day 3, Susan joined me on the river from Greenville to Vicksburg, Mississippi. Susan was a real trouper. She started the trip with the stomach flu and finished it soaking wet in the dark. Not once did she complain.

ABOVE/TOP RIGHT: Preparing for another day on the river in the sweltering heat.

Susan, Jennifer, and I are headed to Vicksburg on Day 3.

Jennifer, the "Ninja" on the river, finally covers up to protect her sunburned skin. She and I carried extra containers of gas tied to the back of the jet skis in case we needed to fuel up along the way.

The river looks calm and inviting, but storms whipped up quickly and challenged our resolve. We didn't flinch.

An old steamboat now used as a riverboat casino in Vicksburg.

Jennifer passing barges parked along the river.

Jennifer and I leave Vicksburg on Day 4.

Flooding along the river has been a huge problem over the years. Here, a flood gauge in Vicksburg shows the various levels.

Jennifer and I remove stones from the jet ski.

Jennifer entertains us on a long day on the river by doing some acrobatics.

Jackie found this abandoned religious shrine and eagerly explored it in Vicksburg. Turns out a man built it for his soon-to-be wife, both now deceased. The former grocery store and home have become a tourist attraction.

We enjoyed so many great meals on our trip, including lunch here at Monsour's (aka Fat Eddie's) in Vicksburg. The chef opened early and cooked a special meal for us.

ABOVE: Jackie, like the rest of us, needed a good breakfast to start the long day.

LEFT: Jennifer picked this spot in Vicksburg: The Cedar Grove Mansion, a 33-room estate that dates back to 1840. Here, she opened up to us.

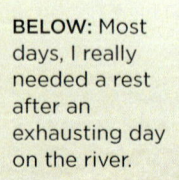

BELOW: Most days, I really needed a rest after an exhausting day on the river.

TOP/ABOVE: The Cedar Grove Mansion offered lots of luxury and relaxation. Our emotional night here really brought us together.

Another great meal: Shrimp etouffee at the Magnolia Grill in Natchez, Mississippi. Southerners know how to cook!

This ornate design is a manhole cover in front of the Magnolia Grill. Susan was amazed by it.

We were more than halfway to New Orleans by the time we reached Natchez.

The Monmouth Inn, a 19th-century, pre-Civil War mansion, sits on 26 acres of gorgeous gardens. We enjoyed the plush accommodations at this member of the Small Luxury Hotels of the World.

Jennifer and the rest of us spent hours laughing, eating, drinking and relaxing at Restaurant 1818 at the inn.

Jackie enjoyed exploring the grounds at the inn. She was much more relaxed on this second leg of our trip.

Susan and I really enjoyed our downtime on the trip. I was so glad to have her with us. And the girls were, too. She was a calming, warm presence for us all.

The grounds at the Monmouth Inn were exquisite: wisteria-covered pergolas, angel statutes, flower gardens and huge, old oak trees.

Dinners were a real form of recovery from the day on the river for us. Drinks and good food were essential fuel for our trip. Here we are at Restaurant 1818 at Monmouth Historic Inn in Natchez.

Getting on the river in Simmesport, Louisiana, en route to Baton Rouge was difficult because of this lock and dam.

The river became very industrial as we got closer to New Orleans.

Between Simmesport and Baton Rouge. Amazingly beautiful when the river is calm.

Baton Rouge was our last stop before New Orleans

Luckily, I never had to use the machete. But it was reassuring to have two of them with us. Here, Jackie brandishes one for the camera.

We never tired of the great food, including here at The Little Village in Baton Rouge.

We are all smiles in Baton Rouge. The next day, we'd get on the river for our final leg to New Orleans.

Jackie read an Allen Ginsberg poem the morning of our last day on the river. It made us all laugh and lightened the mood.

A beautiful sunset on the Mississippi.

The moment we got out of the river in New Orleans.

Victory toast at the Ritz-Carlton in New Orleans. Boy, were we glad to be there!

Music, including from this jazz band, was everywhere you went in New Orleans.

Jackie and Jennifer discover room service! They were soaking up the last days of this trip.

The weather was not the greatest, but we still enjoyed sightseeing in New Orleans.

We had a celebratory dinner at Arnaud's, a fabulous restaurant in the heart of the French Quarter.

Museum at Arnaud's featuring costumes from past Mardi Gras.

At Lafitte's Blacksmith Shop Bar, friends Larry Fischer and Ken Misener wrote about our accomplishment on one of the tables.

Friends Ken and Beth Misener came from Cleveland to celebrate with us in The Big Easy.

Susan and I were so glad to have finished our river journey together. Here, we enjoy lunch at Pierre Maspero's.

Jackie and Jennifer are happy sisters at the Carousel Bar in New Orleans. This trip changed their relationship and helped bring them closer.

Our final meal of the trip: Breakfast with the Miseners and Larry Fischer and his wife, Marlene (right).

The Journey Continues

Chapter 5

Back On The River

Sunday, August 12, 2012
Day 1: Halls, Tennessee, to Memphis, Tennessee

As soon as we hit the dirt road, the trip felt real again.

The girls stood up and popped their heads out of the Jeep and took photos. They leaned out the windows, held up their iPhones and captured videos of each other and the huge trees and swampland around us.

They screamed with excitement.

"It was a wild, wild feeling driving down that dirt road,"

Jennifer said. "It felt like I went through time almost."

We were about 80 miles north of Memphis in Chickasaw National Wildlife Refuge in Halls, Tennessee, a small town in the southwestern corner of the state. And we were headed straight for the Mississippi River.

Despite the remoteness, it felt familiar in both an exciting and painful way.

This was the spot where we ended our first trip down the river five years earlier — about 720 miles short of our final destination, New Orleans.

Now we were back, with a new team and a new determination to finish the mission and reach New Orleans.

Chickasaw National Refuge lies in the Lower Mississippi River floodplain along the Chickasaw Bluff in western Tennessee. It was created in August 1985 and includes the largest block of bottomland hardwood forest in Tennessee.

Bottomland hardwood forests are basically river swamps. They're typical along rivers and streams in the southeast in broad floodplains. They're filled with different species of beautiful Gum, Oak and Bald Cypress trees, which have the ability to survive in areas that are frequently flooded and covered in water.

The trees have a ring around their base — a water mark — that reflects the recent flood levels.

These forests serve a critical purpose by reducing the risk and severity of flooding to nearby communities by storing floodwater.

Throngs of birds — as many as 250,000 during peak times — flock to Chickasaw as a stopover during migration.

As we drove down the dirt road, dust flying up around us, I thought how great it was for the kids to be buying into this adventure again.

We had the radio tuned to a local rock station when a Michael Jackson song came on. Jennifer turned up the volume and she and Jackie sang and moved to the beat. MJ's music always connected those two, despite their differences.

"I was really thankful that we just got to spend time together, the three of us," Jennifer said. "Although I was walking on eggshells and thought that Jackie was going to stab me in the back, we did have a good time and were being really nice to each other."

Jackie had a history of "telling on her sister" and getting her in trouble.

But she was excited to hang out with Jennifer on this trip.

"Jennifer and I were both unsure of how things were going to go," Jackie said. "But I just felt that maybe we had matured enough to get along. I had hope that we would start building a relationship."

Our fourth and newest team member, my girlfriend, Susan Tarry, was back at the hotel, sick in bed.

"I think God took me out," she said. "I woke up at 4 in the morning sick as a dog, flu systems. I was hanging on the toilet.

"There wasn't a chance that I was gonna get on the jet ski that day."

She thought her absence benefitted me and the girls.

"That was really critical that they had that time to themselves the first day," she said. "On the first trip, their family had gotten ripped apart.

"Bill needed this with his daughters. This one day. They are still a family even though it looks different than it did before."

Facebook Brings Us Back Together, LOL

Susan Tarry / September 5, 2011, 6:52pm

Hello Bill! Lyn said you were on Facebook. My daughter "brought me up to speed" in July. How have you been?

Bill Ayars / September 7, 11:51am

Susan, wow, great to hear from you! Where do I begin...well, I live in Bay Village and have 2 daughters. For the most part, didn't stay very connected with many folks from Vermilion, but have found recently that it's been fun to see some [of] the old clan. But enough about me, tell me more about what you have been doing.

This is how my high school sweetheart and I reconnected after not seeing each other for 37 years: Facebook.

We needed coaching and encouragement from our kids since both of us were new to social media. (Jennifer, for example, told me with a chuckle that LOL means Laugh Out Loud and not Lots of Love.)

Susan and I went to Vermilion High School in the 1970s. She was a year younger. We dated during my junior and senior years before I went off to Kent State University to study drafting and then architecture.

With me away at college, we drifted apart.

My Childhood Near the Lake

I moved to Vermilion when I was in first grade.

I was the youngest of four kids — six years younger than my youngest sister. I was the "accident," I think.

We came to Ohio from Michigan, where my dad worked for Ford.

When I was 5, he was transferred to the Ford plant in Lorain, Ohio, where he worked as a quality control manager.

We rented a house in Wakeman for a year before settling in downtown Vermilion. Our house was about a quarter mile from Lake Erie.

By sixth grade, I was the only kid left in the house.

We had a boat, and we would water ski and take trips to the Lake Erie islands.

I focused on fun, not academics, in high school, and my grades suffered.

One class I took seriously, though, was architectural drawing during my junior year. There were seven of us in the class. Four of us went on to become architects.

Bill Ayars / September 7 at 7:51pm
[to Susan Tarry on Facebook]

I started writing and it disappeared. not sure went out or not....I am still a novice at this...I'll try again. 5 grandkids that's unbelievable! On this end Jackie, the 20-year-old, can't wait to have kids and Jennifer, the 23-year-old, will probably never have kids. They are such opposites.

About 9 years ago, a colleague and I put an architectural firm together, so between that, golf, and a couple of jet skis, that fills much of my time. I am single although I was married for quite some time....as I mentioned in my original version, it's hard to believe we are talking about "adult" things and not about skipping school....your turn...tell me more.

Susan Tarry / September 8 at 6:07pm

LOL! I am cracking up! You are right, my youngest daughter is older than we were when we were going out! Weird! Still feel young, though... An architectural firm, huh? Very good! Having your own business does keep you busy, doesn't it? Golf and jet skis, hmmm... I've never been on a jet ski. Seems like fun? I have jumped out of an airplane (a long time ago), gone rock climbing and rappelling, horseback riding, zip lining, and kayaking. Back to you...

As Susan and I exchanged messages, almost daily in those two-and-a-half weeks in September, we began to rekindle our friendship.

There was both a warm familiarity in our exchanges — the memories of my old blue Mustang, the orange juice and ham sandwiches, "fruit loops" that she pulled from my shirt to signal she liked me — and the prospect of an exciting new beginning.

Bill Ayars / September 18 at 8:19am

I know it's a little over the edge...considering that we have just started talking...but I'll say it, I do wish you were here spending time together...hope that doesn't put you in an uncomfortable area, you can tell me if it does....

Susan Tarry / September 18 at 12:21pm
... I am really looking forward to hanging out with you and talking in person. Do really enjoy hearing your laugh on the phone. It hasn't changed a bit.

We chatted about the Mississippi River trip, too.

Bill Ayars / September 9 at 8:05am
... Couple years back we did ride the jet skis down the Mississippi from St.Paul to Memphis...almost 1000 miles. Planned to go the whole way to New Orleans and I am still hoping to finish that trip....need a new adventure?

Susan Tarry / September 9 at 6:06pm
I saw the picture of you and your daughter on the jet skis! Great picture! How long did it take you to go 1000 miles on jet skis?? How fast do they go? Did you camp out? I want to hear more about that!

Onward Down the River

As we neared the end of the dirt road in Chickasaw Refuge on that hot August day in 2012, we could see the ramp and river ahead. We were ready for the second part of our journey.

"I wanted to make a memory with my new family," Jackie said. "I don't think there was a doubt in our minds that we were going to make it to New Orleans. We were going to make it this time, if it killed us."

Jackie again was the navigator, the driver who would make her way through the small, sometimes deserted river towns and find us and the jet skis in the most remote areas.

Jennifer was my river partner, the sometimes-renegade who only wanted to be on the water.

When I stopped the Jeep at the edge of the river, Jennifer jumped out and started getting the gear ready. Life jackets. Paddle. Machetes. (I decided to bring machetes in case we encountered any alligators or snakes along the way.)

Because of a drought that summer, the Mississippi was down about 10 feet.

Just a year earlier, the water levels on the river were near record highs. But this year, the river plunged to a 50-year low.

The water level was so low that the Army Corps of Engineers had to dredge deeper than normal to keep the shipping channel open. Still, barges had to lighten their loads to avoid running aground.

On top of that, the weather was brutally hot and humid. It turned out to be one of the hottest years on record.

For us, the lower water levels and sweltering heat were an inconvenience but not a deterrence. We just had to make adjustments along the way.

So on Day 1, we had to back the trailer — with the skis still on it — onto the rocks and into the water.

Jennifer and I climbed onto the jet skis. Jackie hopped into the Jeep.

Puffy white clouds floated in the blue sky, reflecting in the calm river water. The air was thick and the sun hot.

A typical August day in the south.

Jennifer and I started our engines and waved goodbye to Jackie.

I felt relaxed. The pain and suffering had disappeared.

It felt good to be back on the river.

Chapter 6

Susan Recovers, We Keep Going

Bill told me many times that people said this trip couldn't be done. It was dangerous. There were whirlpools. The wakes created by the tugboats were treacherous. The whole thing is crazy!

So, what did I think?

I think I work in a bank. Life is short and no guarantees. Bill is cautious and big on planning and preparation. And if I die on the Mississippi River, well, that's not all bad. Better than dying in a car crash on the way to work or in a nursing home. Besides,

I didn't think anybody would be dying. And just think of the stories I'd have to tell!

— Susan Tarry, Journal Entry

Susan and I had been dating for nearly two years when my daughters and I decided to finish our Mississippi River trip. I had been thinking about selling the jet skis, but before I did, I asked the girls if they wanted to finish what we had started five years earlier.

To my surprise, they said yes.

We wanted Susan along, too.

Unlike my ex-wife, Susan was excited and eager for our adventure. And she wanted to ride the jet ski, not just follow along in the Jeep.

That put me in a bit of a bind because Jennifer wanted to ride, too. How would we decide who got on the other jet ski with me? We'd figure that out later.

The good news was that both Jennifer and Jackie liked Susan and welcomed her on our team.

"At first, I wanted my mom there in a hurtful, crazy way," Jennifer said. "It kind of made me feel bad that I was on this trip and my mom wasn't."

"So, was it weird that we started this trip with my mom and finished it with Susan? Yeah," she said. "But I love Susan. I don't think there is anybody in the world that could have fit in and dealt with us … Her presence was OK with me."

Jackie, too, embraced Susan.

"I felt really safe with her and felt like I was able to

communicate with her," Jackie said.

"Her coming was a safe zone for me and my sister. I feel like we shouldn't act up in front of her. ... Jennifer would be on her best behavior and I would be on mine."

Keeping the Troops Happy

The girls and I finished the first 80 miles from Halls to Memphis, Tennessee, without a hitch that first day. The weather cooperated and there were no glitches.

We were all feeling pretty good.

"I felt reunited with my adventurous partner when my dad and I got on the river that first morning," Jennifer said. "It was like: 'Hey, remember this? This was something cool we did together.' I really liked that."

Jennifer and Jackie were getting along, too.

"We were actually enjoying each other's company," Jennifer said.

Said Jackie: "The trip is when our first relationship of our lives ever formed."

That evening, Jackie and Jennifer went to dinner together while I stayed back at the hotel with Susan, who was still sick in bed.

Good (expensive) dinners would be a hallmark of this trip. It was almost blackmail: I had to keep the troops happy. Food and drink seemed to work.

That night, Jackie ordered lobster ravioli and Jennifer enjoyed Steak Oscar with scallops and gruyere au gratin potatoes. And of course, they each had a few drinks. The bill was $200.

It was a small price to pay for my daughters enjoying a good meal — and each other's company.

August 13, 2012
Day 2: Memphis, Tennessee, to West Helena, Arkansas

Though Susan was feeling better, she wasn't ready to get on a jet ski. And I wasn't ready to tell Jennifer that it was Susan's turn to ride and she had to ride in the Jeep with Jackie.

"Bill didn't want to confront that situation, telling her that she was going to have to take turns with me," Susan said.

So on Day 2 of our trip, Susan rode in the Jeep with Jackie and Jennifer got back on the river with me.

That day's drive with Susan turned out to be one of the most memorable parts of the trip for Jackie.

She and Susan didn't know each other well because Jackie had moved to Colorado before Susan and I started dating. So this trip was a real opportunity for them to get to know each other better.

Jackie was still scared of the river. She feared one of us — or all of us — would get hurt.

"I just think it's very powerful," she said. "It's a very spiritual, powerful life force. People die on the Mississippi a lot. It's unpredictable and huge."

[There's no authoritative number of total deaths on the river because cities and towns keep their own individual records. But in the Twin Cities alone, there were three deaths on the river in 2012 and at least 10 in 2013, according to the

St. Paul Pioneer Press.]

Jackie shared her fears with Susan as they drove from Memphis to West Helena. Susan, in turn, described a fearful time in her life when she was afraid of her ex-husband.

"One time, she was hiding in the bedroom and she thought he was gonna kill her," Jackie recalled.

Jackie could barely fathom that.

"I was afraid of the dark!" Jackie said. "It gave me a lot of strength to hear her story. She's a real bad ass."

It was the first taste of the calming effect Susan, a Christian, would have on the girls.

"I told the story to Jackie to try to explain my faith in God's ability to love us and protect us," Susan said.

It was one of many frank, open conversations on the trip that would strengthen our team's bond and foster our family's healing.

Gas Up and Go

The planning for this trip was a little easier because I had pretty much mapped it out the first time.

But since then, I realized there were no marinas on this part of the river, which meant no gas stations. And there were fewer ramps, too.

So I spent a lot of time trying to figure out how to get from one ramp to the next on one tank of gas. My calculations were critical because there were no odometers on the jet skis to track mileage.

There was just this annoying, loud beep to signal the

tank was low. The piercing sound scared the shit out of me.

On the first half of our trip in 2007, we usually cruised between 58 and 61 mph. This time, we'd have to slow down to 40 mph to conserve gas and reach our destinations without refueling.

Also, I knew this southern stretch was more remote than up North. I wanted to keep Jackie safe. I didn't want her driving in the middle of nowhere to find us.

So I focused on locating ramps in cities and on the east side of the river because it was more populated.

That made it important to know where the bridges were. There were far fewer on this part of the river than up North.

There was a bridge from tiny Lula, Mississippi (pop: 370 in 2000) to Helena-West Helena, Ark. (pop: 12,282 in 2010), our destination on Day 2.

Lula is just 0.4 square miles and poor. In 2000, the median household income was $23,125; for a family, it was $33,295, according to the U.S. Census. About 39 percent of the population lived below the poverty line, including nearly 60 percent of children.

For Jackie — and really all of us — seeing these small towns and the way these people lived so differently from us was a real eye-opener.

"I had never been down south at all," Jackie said. "That's why I was in shock at these river towns. All these houses on little stilts. It looked like something from a Tom Sawyer movie."

She also found communicating with the locals could be difficult.

"It's like a different language down south," Jackie said. "It's crazy that people who live in the same country, I can't even understand them at times."

Our first day from Halls to Memphis was a test run for our mileage and gas theory. We rode at 40 mph and it worked perfectly.
We made it 80 miles on one tank of gas.

But there were upcoming stretches of our trip that would be longer than that, so we needed a Plan B.
Part of that plan was carrying spare gas containers with us. I bought two 2 ½-gallon containers, filled them with gas and attached them to the back of each of our jet skis with bungee cords. It was our emergency supply.
The manager of the store where I bought the jet skis sort of scrunched his face and said he didn't think towing gas containers was a good idea.
I worried, too, especially about the one tied to Jennifer's ski. But I worried about getting stuck in the middle of the river without gas.
There are mile markers on the river, so that helped. But I had to keep close tabs on our speed and my map.
Riding the river was pretty amazing. Despite the loud jet skis and occasional shrill beeps, it was calming. I fell into a bit of a trance watching the reflections of the sky and trees in the water while I rode.
The river isn't a deep blue or green like the ocean or a

lake. It is the color of the brown mud it mixes with. Susan, when she sat behind me on the jet ski, often stared at the water and noticed the little eddies in the dark water. She watched the way it flowed and changed color.

Despite its muddy color, it was pretty and sometimes mesmerizing.

The shoreline, however, didn't offer much scenery. There was a mix of desolate sandy beaches and small rocky beaches immediately backed by dense woods. Sometimes we saw little dirt roads winding down toward the river, but with no access to it.

Near high ground, it appeared populated. But in the lower areas, the levees separated the river and any activity going on nearby.

Sometimes barges docked by the shore to get filled with grain. That captured our attention for miles as we got closer to them.

Clouds of dust rose up into the air as the grain poured down into them from the silos. The barges floated lopsided in the water as one end filled faster than the other.

It made for different scenery than up North, where we shared the river with recreational boaters near the cities and gazed at a more developed, populated shoreline.

As I looked along the barren, shoreline here, I often wondered who lived near here. What did they do?

The Sights and Sounds of the River

We didn't talk much as we rode because it was nearly

impossible to hear each other over the engines. But it was definitely nice to have a companion on the water.

Still, I felt a sense of isolation on the river, even with a riding partner. At the start of our trip, I assumed we'd see lots of activity throughout our ride. But there wasn't much beyond barge traffic, fishing boats and an occasional steamboat south of Memphis.

To pass the time and stay on course, Susan and I kept a constant lookout for the buoys and mile markers. Both were important: The buoys marked the shipping channel and the mile markers helped us track our gas supply.

Time had a tendency to slow on the river. It seemed to take forever to reach a bridge ahead of us, as it slowly, slowly got larger and larger as we drew near.

There wasn't much wildlife to see, only an occasional cow in the grass or a couple of dogs on the beaches. Some birds, of course, but not many for that much water.

Susan and I listened to the steady drone of the jet skis as we rode.

Jennifer often inserted ear buds and listened to music on her iPhone as we rode. It looked like she was sort of bouncing around the river to the music. It made me smile.

We didn't have iPhones on the first leg in 2007 and they made communicating — and entertaining ourselves — much easier on this trip.

I sent location "pins" from my phone to Jackie's via text, so she could find the ramps by entering our location into the Jeep's GPS. It was much easier than lugging the laptop along and using satellite service.

Still, river maps are different than road maps. They show very little of what was on the nearby land.

So at breakfast each morning, I examined the river map to find a ramp and then searched Google Earth for it so we could locate a pin. Then, I'd forward that pin to Jackie's phone.

On the river, I relied on an important lesson I learned from the first trip: Always stay in the boat channel between the buoys. I also learned, from my pre-trip research, that there could be alligators in the river as far north as Memphis. And I knew snakes could be slithering around nearby, too.

So we brought machetes. I thought about hooking mine to my belt but decided to store it in a container instead. I didn't want to get pulled over by the Department of Natural Resources again.

The second day on Monday was a long haul: 75 miles to West Helena, where we gassed up, then about 80 miles more before we were forced off the river by a bad storm. We drove the remaining 20 miles or so to Greenville, where we stayed for the night.

Jackie sank down to her knees in the mud, digging out a clamshell, while she and Susan waited for us near West Helena. She had to dig out her shoes, too, because they sank next to her.

But she got her prize: a large clamshell, which she modeled — one half over each eye — afterward.

Jennifer came off the river tired and sunburned. She had again refused to wear sunscreen.

We grabbed lunch at a Mexican restaurant in West Helena and then headed back to the river to continue on to Greenville.

We soon discovered the second half of our day would not go as smoothly as the first.

Chapter 7

Move the [Bleeping] Barge!

Monday, August 13, 2012
Day 2 Continued: West Helena, Arkansas, to Greenville, Mississippi

    Sunburned, tired and cranky, Jennifer decided to take a break from the jet ski and ride in the Jeep with Jackie. Susan rode on the river with me.

    It looked like the clouds were disappearing and it was going to be a nice afternoon for our ride. But I knew the skies could change quickly.

    Sure enough, Susan and I got caught in a downpour near

the end of the day.

We wore goggles and wet-weather gear, but the rain still pelted our faces as we rode. We drove slowly because if we went too fast, the rain felt like needles on our skin.

As we neared our ramp, we saw three massive barges parked in front, blocking our way.

I didn't realize until we got on the river how huge the barges are.

A typical barge carries 1,500 tons of cargo, which is 15 times greater than a rail car and 60 times greater than a trailer truck.

Hundreds of millions of tons of cargo are moved on the Mississippi River each year. Barges transport all kinds of goods, but typically it's coal, petro-chemical products and grain.

The barges tend to travel together, forming a river tow. An average river tow on the Upper Mississippi River is 15 barges consisting of five barges tied together and moving three abreast.

The same load hauled on land would require a train three miles long or a line of trucks stretching more than 35 miles.

With our ramp blocked, we anchored near a small beach on the opposite side of the river. We got off the jet skis and waited. It continued to pour, thunder and lightning.

We stood there, soaked.

Across the river near the ramp, we could see the Jeep trying to back up to the ramp.

Susan and I watched as the tail lights went on and off.

On and off. On and off. I'm thinking, "Oh, these kids are not happy!"

The road that led to the ramp was winding and narrow, so it was difficult for Jackie to maneuver the trailer.

"It was two tire tracks through the grass," she said. "It made a dirt road seem luxurious."

After multiple attempts to back up the trailer, Jennifer jumped out of the passenger seat to help. She picked up the trailer and tried to move it into place.

It was a slow process. It took about 30 minutes for them to reach the ramp.

Jackie and Jennifer peered across the half-mile wide river to look for us.

"We saw two little green people far away," Jackie said, referring to our green rain gear.

She wanted the barge to move. She walked to the edge of the ramp and yelled to the people on board: "MOVE THE FUCKING BARGE!"

Jennifer burst out laughing, lightening a frustrating situation.

Someone on the barge yelled back that the jet skis could maneuver around them. The girls encouraged us to give it a try, and Susan and I got back on the jet skis and headed toward the ramp.

We squeezed through but discovered the ramp was slippery and crumbling. I feared the trailer and Jeep would slide back into the river if we tried to load the jet skis there.

Just as we were trying to figure out what to do next, a man

appeared from the nearby woods. He just popped out of the trees. I'm thinking, "What the heck is that guy doing here?"

Turns out he was a lock operator and knew the river well. He got a map from his car and showed us another ramp about five miles downriver.

We thanked him and told the girls to meet us there.

I still wonder about that guy because a girl got off the barge and rode a raft to shore to meet him. "Who the hell meets a barge to pick up women?" I wondered.

We were low on gas but had no choice but to continue. We didn't have the extra gas containers with us, so there was no backup.

The jet skis beeped periodically as we rode, reminding us of our precarious situation.

We overshot the ramp because we missed the inlet leading to it. Fortunately, Susan looked back and saw a tugboat exiting there and we turned around.

Once at the ramp, I sent a pin locator to Jackie. They showed up about 20 minutes later.

Love It or Hate It, We Made it to Greenville

Susan and I were happy to be back on land. Wet, tired and hungry, we headed to our accommodations for the night at The Greenville Inn and Suites to get cleaned up for dinner at the only place we found open in town: a Chinese buffet.

It's funny that we wound up at a buffet because I had to avoid them during my chemo. Too many germs, I guess.

It was the only reasonably priced dinner we'd have on

the trip.

Greenville was a different place for us. Its downtown was dilapidated and filled with boarded-up and graffitied buildings.

"It was so depressing," Jennifer said. "It made me so sad to see this forgotten place. These people were forgotten souls."

Greenville, which had a population of about 34,000 in 2010, according to the U.S. Census, had been through some tragic times.

Before the Civil War, the original city was a thriving settlement that was a cultural and business center for the large cotton plantations that surrounded it.

But during the siege of nearby Vicksburg, Union troops burned down every building in Greenville.

That forced residents to relocate and rebuild at its current location, three miles away. Greenville now sits on the highest point on the Mississippi River between Vicksburg and Memphis.

But after the rebuilding, in 1877, yellow fever decimated the community by killing a third of its 1,000 residents, including the mayor and four of its five councilmen.

A resilient group later organized a cotton exchange and cotton — which grew so well because of the rich Delta soil — brought prosperity to the city.

But flooding knocked the city down again. Thirteen years later, in 1890, water covered half of Greenville.

It rebounded again and enjoyed nearly three decades of growth before a levee broke eight miles north. Ten feet of water rushed in, completely covering the Delta for three months.

It was one of the greatest natural disasters in U.S. history.

Greenville has some proud history, too: In the 20th century, more than 100 published writers, including Shelby Foote, Hodding Carter and Walker Percy, called the city home — more than any town of its size in the country.

Muppet creator Jim Henson also was born in Greenville in 1936 and raised nearby.

Puddin' and the Glass Bottles

While Jennifer disliked Greenville, Jackie embraced it.

The night we arrived, Jackie stood outside and took video of a lightning storm that lit up the dark sky. She was fascinated by it.

She also wandered around near the inn and discovered hundreds of glass bottles in a warehouse across the street. She loves glass.

"I was gonna break in and grab two of them but decided to wait until the next morning," she said with a chuckle.

That morning, she saw the garage door to the warehouse open and walked in. She met owner Puddin Moore, who collects glass bottles from throughout Mississippi.

She was impressed to learn that he was featured on the History Channel's "American Pickers" show. The show shares stories of people who turn trash into treasure.

Jackie stayed and talked to Puddin' for more than an hour.

"I couldn't pull myself out of conversation with this guy," she said. "Dad was freaking out because he couldn't find me."

Jennifer, on the other hand, couldn't leave Greenville fast enough. She was crabby the first few days of our trip and it bubbled over in Greenville.

She cried. She withdrew. She called her girlfriend, Andrea, and sobbed to her.

At dinner that night and again at breakfast the next morning, she said she wanted to go home.

She had been upset when we chose The Greenville Inn for our accommodations, but Susan told her, nicely but firmly, to deal with it.

"Susan hurt my feelings and I took it super personally," Jennifer said.

But we soon discovered that it was much more than bruised feelings eating at Jennifer.

Chapter 8

Jennifer Opens Up

Tuesday, August 14, 2012

Day 3: Greenville to Vicksburg, Mississippi

Jennifer, although melancholy and moody, decided she wanted to get back on the river. Susan wanted to ride on the jet ski again, too.

I didn't want to disappoint either of them, so all three of us rode. Susan sat on the back of my ski.

Fortunately, it was a shorter trip than the previous day, especially for Jackie. It took her only 90 minutes to drive to

Vicksburg. That left her with several hours to kill before we arrived.

"That was one of my favorite days of the trip," she said. "I had so much time to explore."

She drove south on Route 61, which is part of the famous "Blues Trail." This stretch of the highway got its nickname because it holds an important place in blues music, serving both as a popular lyrical symbol for travel and as the actual route many artists used to travel north.

Bob Dylan sang about the highway in his famous 1965 song "Highway 61 Revisited" on the album of the same name.

Several African-American singers and musicians lived along the southern stretch of Highway 61 in Mississippi, including Muddy Waters, the Ealey brothers, Polka Dot Slim and Percy Strother.

Along Route 61, Jackie also spent time exploring what she described as an abandoned, rundown, Jesus-worshipping commune just north of Vicksburg. The locals know it as the former Margaret's Grocery store or H.D. Dennis's roadside religious shrine.

"It was the weirdest thing I'd ever seen," Jackie said.

There was a large, brick archway painted red, white, yellow and pink leading to the old, abandoned grocery store. Nearby sat a broken-down bus with its side panels painted pink, white and green. A sign in front of it read: "THIS IS THE HOUSE OF PRAYER FOR THE CHURCH PEOPLE TO WORSHIP THE LORD PLEASE READ THIS — ThANKS"

The bricks and cinder blocks around the building were painted yellow and pink, and red and white.

Jackie snapped photos and posted them on Facebook. Almost immediately, her cell phone rang.

"Where the hell are you? Where's your dad? Get out of there!" the concerned voice on the other end said.

"Hi Mom," Jackie said.

The site, although alarming to Jackie's mother, is a well-known folk art attraction and the work of the late Rev. H.D. Dennis, who promised Margaret, the grocery store owner: "If you marry me, I'll turn your store into a palace."

Margaret Rogers Dennis, now deceased, had owned the grocery store for nearly 40 years when she married Rev. Dennis in 1984.

The couple used red, white, pink and yellow painted concrete blocks, scrap-iron columns, foam balls and other everyday items to create the place, which they considered their castle. Mardi Gras beads, plastic trinkets and Christmas lights decorated much of the inside.

Hand-painted signs featured religious phrases such as: "It is written my house shall be called the house of prayer but ye have made a den of thieves."

As Jackie explored the folk art palace, Susan, Jennifer and I cruised down the river. We had the extra gas containers this time, in case we needed to refuel on the river.

It was a clear, sunny day, so the riding was fun and easy.

Jennifer chased a steamboat and did "tricks" on her jet ski; she motioned for Susan to watch.

She sat, laid flat on her stomach and jumped up and stood on her jet ski — all while flying down the river. Susan laughed and caught all of it on video as she and I rode alongside Jennifer.

After baking in the sun awhile, Jennifer finally stopped to cover up. She wrapped special cooling bandanas around her head and face. Susan and I nicknamed her Ninja Skier.

"It looked like I was about to rob a gas station," Jennifer said.

As always, large barges accompanied us down the river. We steered around them and carefully navigated the large waves they created in their wake.

The scenery wasn't nearly as nice as it had been up North, on our first leg of the trip. The rolling land and green landscape were gone, replaced with commercial and industrial landscape.

Only a handful of bridges carried cars and trucks over the river.

In Mississippi, there were four operable bridges that crossed the river at the time of our trip: the Greenville Bridge, the Helena Bridge, Vicksburg Bridge and Natchez Vidalia Bridge. These crossings were important because they were the only ones that could take Jackie across the river in the Jeep if she needed to reach us on the opposite side.

As she entertained us with her jet-ski tricks, Jennifer appeared happy and carefree. But inside, she was agitated and angry.

"I was just not feeling good," she said later. "Throughout

the whole ride down the river, I was getting more and more worked up."

The Mansion

On land, Jackie was agitated, too, but for a different reason. As she waited, alone and uncertain of what was taking us so long , her fears took hold.

"I thought they blew up," she said, imagining a crash that ignited the extra gas containers.

But we made it safely to Vicksburg and I vowed then to keep in better touch with Jackie during the rest of the trip to help ease her anxiety.

We headed to the Cedar Grove Mansion, a historic, old inn that Jennifer had chosen.

The girls were in charge of choosing our accommodations, and it seemed each night, the places got more expensive.

The mansion sits on five acres of beautiful gardens, and its 33 rooms and suites are spread throughout five gorgeous buildings.

The place dates to 1840 and was built by wealthy businessman John Alexander Klein. In 1842, at age 40, he married 16-year-old Elizabeth Bartley Day.

On their year-long honeymoon in Europe, Klein bought much of the furniture that's still at the inn. The mansion, which features Italian marble fireplaces and large gold-leaf mirrors, was completed in 1852.

During the Civil War, a cannonball was fired into the parlor and lodged in the wall. It's still there today. The mansion survived the attacks during the war largely because it served as a Union hospital.

We ate lunch at Monsour's and then went back to the mansion to relax and wander around the grounds that were filled with green, rolling lawns and bright, beautiful gardens. The gardens were filled with flowering Crape Myrtle trees, ferns and statues.

There was a small cemetery on the grounds and a pool with statues of lions at each corner, serving as fountains.

Out back, a brick patio with wrought iron tables and chairs invited guests to sit and enjoy the view. Jackie relaxed there and wrote in her journal while Susan explored the main house.

We had our choice of rooms in the main house or carriage house. We chose the smaller, two-story carriage house, which had a porch with wrought iron railings and ceiling fans that worked to cut through the humidity.

We stayed on the second floor, Susan and me in one room and the girls in another.

We ate dinner at the inn and afterward, when the bar closed, we headed outside to the veranda. There was a bench and two chairs. Jackie and I sat next to each other on the bench. Jennifer sat on the wicker chair to our left and Susan on the one to our right, forming a small, family circle.

During our trip, evenings had become about recovery. Jackie initially instituted a rule that we could not talk about our day during dinner for more than a few minutes.

"It wasn't going to be all business," she said.

But the rule was short-lived. Some nights, we talked a lot about our journey: venting about a tough day, laughing about a silly one or smiling about a victorious one.

We shared stories and old memories, too.

Susan told the girls about our days as high school sweethearts. We all laughed about the time she gave me a drain plug from a bathtub on the Queen Mary as a gift. (She took it during an overnight stay on the famous boat on a summer vacation.)

"We talked about anything and everything," Susan said.

"We needed that as therapy," Jennifer said.

Especially on this night for Jennifer.

As we sat on the veranda, we could feel the hot, sticky air on our skin. Jackie sipped a glass of red wine. I drank a Manhattan from a glass wet with condensation. Susan enjoyed a cold bottle of Corona with lime.

As we talked, Jennifer began to cry. She realized she had been grumpy and unkind the past couple of days and apologized to us for her behavior.

Susan began to gently but firmly push and prod Jennifer to open up. Soon, what was bothering Jennifer began to spill out.

She told us she was daydreaming about drugs on the river and thinking that her sole motivation for this trip was to be able to drink — a lot. She wondered why she was feeling like this.

"I think I was full of rage because it was the first time we had all been together since I quit doing drugs," she said.

Her addiction had taken control of her back home in Bay Village. She was using all kinds of heavily addictive, dangerous drugs.

With my divorce and my focus on trying to keep moving forward, I didn't notice the changes in her until it came to a head when she ended up in the hospital from an overdose.

I didn't understand what was going on — maybe even pretended it wasn't happening — and had no idea how to help.

Shortly after her overdose, Jennifer moved to Phoenix to live near her mother and work at a restaurant Nancy owned.

"I was a total mess ... and needed a different environment," Jennifer said.

Since arriving in Phoenix, she had been sober.

But being back together with Susan, Jackie and me reminded her of her drug use. She said she felt a desire — almost a pull — to do drugs again.

"I believe what triggered my emotions was being in the same situation that I was last doing drugs in," she said. "Had we not been isolated from society and not been forced to be on the river, I wouldn't have thought twice about acquiring or doing drugs. That's a scary thing to have to come to terms with."

I sat back and listened. I was surprised by her openness. She had never talked about any of this. I guess I didn't look at her drug use as an addiction. I thought it was just partying. Or maybe that's what I wanted to believe.

My normal response would have been to tell Jennifer

how to fix this. But my therapist, whom I had seen during my divorce, told me that most kids don't want you to fix things for them; they just want you to listen.

So that's what I did on this night. And Jennifer noticed.

"This is the first time my dad hadn't said, 'Look this is what you're going to do. This is how it's going to happen.' For the first time, it was like, 'Well, I can tell you how I feel about that, what I would do.' That caught my attention."

We were all empathetic, even Jackie, who usually was hard on her sister.

"When she gets stressed out or something triggers her, her immediate response is to get away, to leave the situation," Jackie said. "I never understood why she'd get so frustrated and just want to get away from us.

"But that night, we sat around and talked about it. When she gets around the family, it stresses her out and makes her want to do drugs and drink. She opened up and talked to us about it, and I was able to understand.

"It changed my perspective. I'm going to support her instead of egging her on or poking her about her anxieties …"

As we talked, Jennifer stopped crying and we all gave her a hug. For the first time, she realized she would have to fight her addiction for the rest of her life. But she realized now that she wouldn't have to do it alone.

"Just hearing someone say: 'We're not judging you still for that' made me feel better," Jennifer said. "Jackie was super supportive. I didn't feel alone."

After that, the tone of the trip changed. A heavy emotional

weight had been lifted. We all felt stronger, closer, more determined to find solutions — together — to the obstacles in front of us.

"That was the night we really decided as a team: We've got this," Susan said. "We'll make this trip what we want it to be. Not just a version of the first trip. This is our trip."

Chapter 9

Rocky Ride

Wednesday, August 14, 2012
Day 4: Vicksburg to Natchez, Mississippi

    After an emotional night, we were ready for a calm, fun day on the river. We were feeling more energized and in sync.

    We were in a groove now.

    We ate breakfast at a little restaurant in the main house. As always, I studied the maps while the girls talked and relaxed.

    Before we got on the river, we removed rocks that were lodged in the propeller of the jet skis from our trip the day before.

I was getting more excited as we neared our final destination, New Orleans.

Jennifer and I planned to ride the jet skis again as we left Vicksburg and headed for Natchez, the oldest city on the Mississippi River.

Natchez, founded in 1716, is known as the birthplace of Mississippi. It sits on a bluff overlooking the river.

The city got its name from its first inhabitants, the Natchez Indians. French explorers arrived next and made it their home in harmony with the Indians.

The French brought slaves from western Africa. They were members of the Bambara tribe, whose name means "those who accept no master." They were the first Africans in Mississippi, and they contributed greatly to the development of Natchez.

English and Spanish residents soon joined the French. Together, they began to build homes and other structures in their native countries' styles, leaving an architectural imprint still characteristic of the city today.

A Quiet Ride

Jennifer and I had an uneventful ride down the river. The trip in the Jeep was quiet for Susan and Jackie, too. As they neared the ramp to pick us up, Jackie saw a sign for an old golf and country club.

She wanted to stop and explore, but the girls had agreed to meet at the ramp before anyone took a side trip.

Once we got the jet skis out of the water and onto the

trailer, we decided to stop and explore the club, which had been closed for years.

The Belwood Golf & Country Club opened in 1967 but was eventually closed because of flooding on the low-lying property. Since then, dozens of trees have been removed from the county-owned property to make room for a levee and commercial development on the site.

We headed to town afterward and ate at the Magnolia Grill on Silver Street, which sits on the river in the Historic Natchez Under-the-Hill District. The area was once home to gamblers, prostitutes and notorious criminals.

Today, it is a popular area for both locals and tourists and includes the Magnolia Grill, the Under-the-Hill Saloon, the city's only riverboat casino and several historic buildings.

The view from the restaurant was great, and we enjoyed more wonderful southern food. Susan had crawfish etouffee and snapped a photo to remember the luscious dish.

The Magnolia Grill was also the place where Susan took one of my favorite photos on the trip: a shot of me, Jackie and Jennifer at the table. I love Jackie's wide-brimmed North Face hat!

That night, we stayed at the Monmouth Historic Inn, a 19th-century, pre-Civil War mansion set on 26 acres of gorgeous gardens. It's a national historic landmark and a member of the Small Luxury Hotels of the World.

The main house is a mansion with four large, white columns in front that support a two-story gallery. There are seven more buildings on the property.

The girls chose a suite in a small building next to the main house, which featured a large, blue canopy bed.

The place was built in 1818 by a couple from Monmouth, New Jersey, which is where it got its name. But they died shortly after moving in.

In 1826, John A. Quitman and his wife, Eliza Turner Quitman, bought the place.

Quitman had arrived in Natchez with a law degree but little money. By marrying Eliza, he joined one of the area's most prominent families and went on to become a partner in the town's most successful law firm.

Quitman later became a general and military hero in the nation's war with Mexico. He also served as governor of Mississippi and as a U.S. Congressman.

Quitman died at Monmouth in the summer of 1858, apparently a victim of what was then known as National Hotel Disease, an illness similar to Legionnaire's Disease. Many American politicians contracted National Hotel Disease after staying or dining at the National Hotel in Washington, D.C.

Quitman's wife died a year later and was buried next to him at Monmouth in the family cemetery. (Quitman's daughters later moved their parents to the city cemetery north of town.)

Susan and Jackie enjoyed exploring the grounds, including the family cemetery that featured an area dedicated to the family dogs. The grounds were exquisite and featured wisteria-covered pergolas, angel statues, bright, blooming flower gardens and huge, old oak trees covered with Spanish moss. There was also a mausoleum.

After a relaxing afternoon, we ate dinner at the hotel's Restaurant 1818, which we had all to ourselves. We spent hours eating, drinking, laughing. The conversation was much lighter than the night before.

It was a wonderful evening.

We had no idea that the next two days would be the most challenging of the trip.

Chapter 10

Mud Man

Thursday, August 15, 2012

Day 5: Natchez, Mississippi, to Baton Rouge, Louisiana (via Simmesport)

For the first time, Jackie agreed to ride the jet skis with me.

"It was the one day that Dad could get me to go on with him," Jackie said. "I wasn't that scared."

Jackie and I posed for pictures before we got on the river: me in my Indiana Jones hat and Jackie with a machete. A couple of hams.

I was excited to ride the river with her.

It was a scorcher that day. Nearly 100 degrees. We had a long trek ahead of us and needed to stop to refuel along the way.

I had located a ramp in Simmesport, Louisiana, where we could get gas.

Simmesport, a town of about 2,100 people, sits at the juncture of the Red and Atchafalaya rivers, which connect by a channel to the Mississippi.

Like many of the other places along our route, Simmesport and the Red River hold an important place in Civil War history.

The Red River was the site of the Union-led Red River Campaign, a series of battles fought along the river from March to May, 1864.

The campaign was a deviation from General Ulysses Grant's original focus on capturing Mobile, Alabama.

During the river battles, the Confederate army successfully defended the Red River Valley with fewer troops than the Union army.

Are Those Asian Carp?

Today, our enemies were the heat, the locks and low water levels near the ramps.

Despite my morning routine of meticulously locating the day's ramps on my map, I couldn't find the one near Simmesport. It was hidden near a lock and dam, which prevented the Mississippi River from jumping over to the

Red River. If the two rivers intersected because of a spillover during a flood, there would be no way to return them to their original paths.

I studied my map for ramps as Jackie and I floated on our jet skis. We saw a fisherman in a small boat and rode over to him. I asked if he could point us to another ramp. He told us there was one back around the bend.

Because of Susan's poor cell service, I couldn't reach her by phone or send her a pin to let her know we were headed to a new ramp.

But when Susan and Jennifer arrived at the area where they thought the ramp should be, they couldn't find it either.

So they drove toward downtown Simmesport to ask if anyone knew of another ramp. There wasn't much there. Just an old gas station and restaurant. They stopped there but no one could direct them to a ramp.

They got back in the Jeep and headed back to the ramp to see if there was indeed a way off the river, which perhaps they missed the first time.

They saw an Army Corps of Engineers facility, which was surrounded by a barbed wire fence.

They pulled up to the front gate. An employee approached them.

They explained they were looking for two jet skiers at a ramp. The man told them no one was there and they couldn't come in.

But Susan and Jennifer pleaded with him to open the gate so they could check for themselves. He finally relented and let them in. But instead of taking them to the ramp, he showed them a video camera view of it. Jackie and I were not there.

Still unconvinced, Susan and Jennifer asked to see the ramp. He drove them in his truck. Jackie and I were not there.

Susan wondered where we could be.

She asked the worker if he knew of another ramp nearby. He did and directed them to it. Meanwhile, Jackie and I were approaching the new ramp.

Turns out it was in a small cove and I worried about the low water levels, which had caused us trouble earlier in the trip. I watched the water carefully as I headed toward the ramp, trying to navigate the low water. Jackie followed closely behind.

"I was so excited to get off of the jet ski," Jackie said.

Then, suddenly, I heard her panicked voice.

"Dad, are those Asian Carp!" she screamed. "Get me the hell out of here!"

I turned around and saw Asian carp jumping out of the water behind her. Asian carp are large fish, sometimes 100 pounds or more. The silver carp species are known to suddenly jump out of the water and injure passing boaters and damage their boats.

"They scared the shit out of me," Jackie said "I'm thinking if I have to get in that water, I will die."

Just then, her jet ski conked out. She had hit a sand bar.

As soon as her engine stopped, the carp stopped jumping. (Apparently, it's the sound of the motor that attracts them.)

I paddled out to Jackie on my jet ski. We were about 50 yards from the ramp. I attached a rope to her jet ski and towed her in.

It was a mucky area with lots of weeds along the shoreline. I was worried about snakes. I hate snakes!

We waited anxiously for about 30 minutes until Susan and Jennifer arrived. As we loaded the skis onto the trailer, we realized there were rocks stuck in Jackie's jet ski.

We found a gas station and restaurant nearby. A woman who worked there said her husband had tools to help us unclog the jet ski. She called him and he came to help us.

It was sweltering out and he did his best to unclog the pipes, but it was Jennifer who was the hero that day. She managed to get the rocks out.

By the time we gassed up the skis, ate lunch and removed the rocks from the exhaust pipe, hours had passed. It felt even hotter now.

We headed back to the ramp to ride the rest of the way to Baton Rouge. Jackie did not want back on the skis. She was done.

Both Susan and Jennifer wanted to ride, so Susan got on with me and Jennifer took the other jet ski. We paddled out in the shallow water.

"Don't go to the right, stay to the left," Jackie shouted. "That's where I got stuck."

But I went to the right. And the jet ski started to sound funny.

Crap. Jackie was right.

I worried it wouldn't make it to Baton Rouge, and we didn't have time to try to fix it. So I hopped on Jennifer's jet ski and asked Susan to take the other one back to land.

Susan gunned the engine and headed back to the ramp. Jennifer and I waited until she and Jackie got the jet ski on the trailer. Then we took off.

Fortunately, we didn't run into any major obstacles during our ride.

Nearly in Tears

We were eager to get off the river when we reached Baton Rouge. But a quick exit eluded us — again.

The ramp was near a bridge, and Jackie and Susan couldn't find it. After navigating through rush hour traffic in Baton Rouge, they searched near the bridge. No ramp.

They stopped a police officer to ask him if he knew where it was. He told them it was near a fish market. Still, they couldn't find it.

They drove back and forth, back and forth, back and forth.

"I was just about ready to come unglued," Susan said. "I was just about in tears talking to Bill on the phone. He was like: Just go up and over the bridge."

But Susan still couldn't find us.

"I was just ready to lose it….." she said.

Just then, I reached the top of the hill from the ramp and walked into the street. Susan and Jackie pulled around the corner.

"Oh my God, I see you!" Susan shouted into the phone.

I was a mess: barechested, muddy and wet.

I jumped into the driver's seat and drove over the sidewalk and grass and past the "No Vehicles Allowed" sign and toward the ramp. Jennifer was with the jet skis, wearing my shirt. She was severely sunburned.

"I was sitting on my jet ski baking and starting to feel really, really sick," she said.

Once on land, she looked down at her arms and nearly gasped.

"There were like a million little bumps on my arm, almost like beads of water," she said. "I went to brush them off and they popped. My skin just came right off. I had ridiculous burns from the sun. It was really bad."

After we loaded the jet ski and got on the road, we burst into laughter and cheers.

We made it!

We headed straight for the Hotel Indigo in downtown Baton Rouge, a contemporary, boutique hotel quite different from the old, historic ones where we had stayed the previous nights.

We were quite a sight pulling up to the valet, who was working his first day on the job.

"We pull up with the Jeep and the trailer and two mud-covered jet skis," Susan said. "Bill was in the front seat with no shirt on, covered with mud.

"We were just all a mess and we go inside this fancy hotel."

They asked us what we were doing. We told them we

were riding jet skis down the Mississippi.

"You're what?" they responded.

One woman in particular stared in disbelief.

"That's impossible," she said. "The undertows! The barges!"

After we showered and cleaned up, we ate dinner at the nearby Little Village Restaurant.

The comments from the locals at the hotel left the girls with some trepidation about our final day on the river.

Jackie said she didn't think we should ride the jet skis into New Orleans because of the dangerous, strong currents where the Mississippi meets the Gulf of Mexico in New Orleans. She suggested we drive instead.

Besides, she said, the locals said there were no ramps to get the skis out.

"I don't give a shit," I said. "I'll leave them in the river."

But before we made any decisions about the final leg, we wanted to enjoy our victory today. We reminisced about it while I recorded the conversation on my iPhone.

"My day was, one word, stressful," Jackie said. "But also, at the same time, it was full of camaraderie because no one was upset at the end of the day, which was the most important thing.

"Also, I saw my dad do something illegal [driving on the sidewalk], so it made up for everything shitty."

Everyone chuckled. Then Jennifer chimed in.

"I liked it," she said. "Yeah, I liked it. I'm not going to lie. Everybody's going to be mad at me [for liking it]. It was stressful, but at the end of the day I feel as if we triumphed.

"I think that we were all happy that we succeeded and that's better than having a boring day and nobody feeling any different. I feel like a survivor today."

I asked Susan if she had any thoughts.

She laughed and asked if she could swear on the video.

"This one took me to the edge," she said. "I nearly cried before we hit leg two, and then leg two was stressful, too. But seeing you bare-chested, with your hat on, mud everywhere, standing on the street corner of Baton Rouge? Baby!"

We all laughed.

Then it was my turn.

"We got stuck in the mud, we ended up on one jet ski. It was pretty challenging," I said. "I thank the team!"

Before we turned the recorder off, Jackie had one more thing to add.

"I heard Susan say, 'Fuck!' for the first time today," she said as the table erupted in laughter.

"I heard it, too," Jennifer said before turning more serious.

"Can I say, throughout this whole trip, THE most amazing part of it all is that Jackie and I have been an exceptional team together," she said.

"I agree," Jackie said.

"We've gotten along the entire time," Jennifer said. "We're kind of the most badass part of the team. I think we've all pulled together as a team. I'm really happy Jackie and I are getting along."

"Cheers," Jackie said. "Love you."

"Cheers!" Jennifer said. "Love you guys."

The day had started out easy, but turned into the hardest day so far.

But I felt good. Unlike the first trip, the chaos didn't rip us apart; it brought us together.

We were truly a team.

Chapter 11

We Made It, Baby! Almost...

Friday, August 16, 2012
Day 6, Baton Rouge to New Orleans

"If you are going to die, it might as well be on a jet ski on the Mississippi..."

— Susan to her friends before leaving for the trip

We woke up to sunshine the morning of our last day on the river.

But the nice weather didn't calm Susan.

She was worried because of the trouble we had exiting the river the day before.

"You need to tell me that this is going to be OK," she said to me as we were getting ready in our hotel room.

"It will be fine," I told her.

"No, you need to look me in the eye and tell me this is going to be OK," she said.

"It will be OK," I said and hugged her.

We gathered with the girls in front of the hotel for coffee. I studied the map to find a ramp to get on the river.

Jackie read a poem from Allen Ginsberg's "The Book of Martyrdom and the Artifice," which she bought earlier in the trip. It contained a passage about poop.

We all chuckled.

"My poetry was my way of trying to keep it fun and not so intense," Jackie said.

Bill, the valet, entertained us, too, by asking our names and then attempting to explain what each one meant.

It was a fun, lighthearted way to start the day.

Who's on the Jet Ski?

I identified a ramp across the river in Port Allen, a city in West Baton Rouge Parish. (A parish is akin to a county.)

But when we arrived there, we found a lock blocking our way to the ramp. We couldn't figure out how to get around it.

We called the Coast Guard and talked to the major of

the flotilla, a head-honcho there. He directed us back to the same "illegal" ramp we arrived at the day before.

So much for trying to obey the law.

The plan was for Susan to ride the ski with me until we stopped for gas; then Jennifer would ride the rest of the way into New Orleans.

Jennifer didn't like the plan.

"I was mad because I felt Susan usurped me and because my dad said he was happy to have her ride with him," she said.

But Jennifer was so sunburned, she needed time off the river. Plus, she injured her back trying to get the jet ski out of the river the day before. She needed rest.

"I thought, 'I could be childish and make this miserable because I had to ride in the car with Jackie on the last day,'" Jennifer said. "But then I thought, 'There's no time to be selfish about petty things like that when we've got a common goal.'"

When we finally reached the ramp, Susan and I got on the one working jet ski. The other ski was out of commission, after sucking up too many rocks the day before.

Jennifer and Jackie jumped in the Jeep and said goodbye. The previous few days set a good tone for their day in the car together.

"We were getting along, which is monumental," Jennifer said. "I'd been trying to build some sort of relationship with her for so long."

Driving Rain, Foggy Goggles and Warning Lights

Our first leg was pretty uneventful — until we reached

the area where the ramp was supposed to be.

The girls told us they couldn't drive there in the Jeep. I didn't know if floodwaters had washed away the road leading to the river or they were just having navigation problems, but they insisted they couldn't see it.

And neither could we.

So we used Susan's phone to find a local road map. We tried to compare it to our river map, so we could find a place to meet.

We found a road a little ways from the river. I told the girls to meet us there.

I parked the jet ski next to the shore, and Susan and I started walking up a bluff covered with tall grass. I feared snakes were hiding in there and regretted that I left the machete in the broken-down jet ski.

Have I mentioned I'm scared to death of snakes?

We carried the gas cans with us, so the girls could go fill them up. It was getting darker and darker; a storm was brewing.

We found the girls, gave them the gas cans and waited for them to return.

They found a mom-and-pop gas station and convenience store in a tiny town. The gas was expensive, although I don't remember how much. I do recall the girls referred to it as highway robbery.

"People were looking at us like we were Paris Hilton," Jennifer said.

The fuel stop took 90 minutes, much longer than we

anticipated. We still had 75 miles to go, which we would barely make — even with the extra fuel — if my mileage calculations were correct.

Jennifer had decided during the morning ride not to join me on the jet ski for the final leg; her back still hurt too much.

So Susan and I would finish the journey into New Orleans.

As we poured gas into the fuel tank, the chain that secured the gas cap broke off and the cap flew into the river. Susan leaped over the ski and grabbed it before it floated away. We quickly screwed it back on and took off.

It was raining now and we could see a storm brewing in the distance.

We rode slowly because our goggles kept fogging up, making it difficult for us to see.

Soon, the storm picked up. Rain. Thunder. Lightning.

There were white caps everywhere. Waves crashed down all round us. The jet ski engine was working hard. We could hear it balking. It sounded like it was on the verge of stalling.

We were in the middle of the river, which is about a mile-and-a-half wide, when I glanced toward shore and spotted a beach. Susan knew what I was thinking: Maybe we should stop.

But then what? We're stuck. There are no roads. There are all sorts of critters.

I quickly realized there was no way off the river here. Susan yelled to me to keep going. I nodded.

A High Voltage light started blinking on the dashboard that I'd never seen before. It flashed every five minutes or so, and I wondered if the jet ski was about to die.

I stayed inside the boating channel but as close to the shore as I could, just in case we needed to paddle or swim to land.

As the lightning flashed, it looked like it was in front of us. But it was hard to be sure because the river kept twisting and turning.

It was spooky.

Susan started praying silently: "OK, God, here's the thing. I know we're idiots to be on this river, but please make this storm stop. Part the clouds, make the lighting stop."

Within a few minutes, the rain slowed but the waves were still rough.

The jet ski went upppp … then crashed down. Uppppp … then crashed down. The engine was straining.

"What I need now is for these waves to calm down!" I yelled back at Susan.

Susan started praying again: "OK, God, you heard him. He needs the waves to stop."

Soon, they, too, calmed down.

We were near New Orleans now. Everything looked industrial. We passed enormous barges and freighters that made even more waves for us to navigate.

We saw a ramp a few miles from New Orleans, but our goal was to get to the River Walk downtown. We kept going.

It was dreary and drizzling when we finally arrived at the River Walk.

Susan took out her iPhone to capture our arrival on video.

She panned the area. The water level was way below street level, exposing the tall beams that held up the River Walk.

"Baby, smile. We made it!" Susan said, pointing the phone at me. Her voice was full of relief.

Then she turned the phone on herself. Her hair was soaked and her glasses covered with beads of water.

"We made it!" she said gleefully. "It was a brutal trip but we are here! Woo-hoo!"

Our glee was soon tempered by the realization that there was no way off the river. There were no ramps, and we couldn't dock at the boardwalk because it was 15-20 feet above our heads. The water level was unusually low because of the recent drought.

Our gas was low, too, so we decided to return to the ramp we had passed a few miles earlier. From there, we could drive to New Orleans.

I was OK with that. We had achieved our goal of making it to New Orleans. Now we just had to find a way to get off the river.

On our way to the ramp, the low gas signal kept beeping, making that shrill, ear-piercing sound.

It unnerved us but we figured we could hold on for a few more miles.

We had no idea then that our journey would last several more hours into the darkness of the night.

Chapter 12

A Light in the Night, Then Screams

As we approached the ramp, Susan sent our pin location to the girls.

When we arrived, I stayed with the jet ski while Susan walked up the hill to figure out where we were. She saw a "No trespassing" sign to her left and then another up ahead. She saw a helicopter pad and a barbed wire fence.

Another U.S. Army Corps of Engineers station.

An armed guard in camouflage gear greeted her at the top of the ramp. She explained to him that we wanted to get the ski out of the river because we were nearly out of gas and couldn't find another ramp.

He was unsympathetic.

"Get back on the jet ski and go," he said.

"We can't. We're almost out of gas," Susan said.

"You can't get out here," he said.

Susan told him we would be gone in five minutes.

He held his gun firmly at his side and said, "Get back on the jet ski and go."

Susan wanted to cry but didn't think it would help. Plus, she had her pride. She quickly returned to the jet ski. I poured what little gas we had left in the gas container into the tank as the guard watched intently.

I started up the jet ski and we headed back toward New Orleans.

The Creepy Drawbridge

It was about 5 p.m. when we arrived in New Orleans for a second time. We saw a police-boat station on the shore and idled outside for a few minutes, waiting for someone to come out and help.

The dock was too high to climb or lift the jet ski out of the water.

A man finally walked out and told us the station did not have a ramp. He directed us to an inlet river that leads to Lake Pontchartrain, a nearby lake that covers 630 square miles. There were marinas and ramps there, he said.

He told us we needed to stay to the left when the river split up ahead, since the right side would take us toward the Gulf of Mexico.

We called the girls, who were relieved to hear from us. They told us they found a ramp at a marina on the inlet river.

That was the good news.

The bad news was that we would have to pass through a lock to get there.

As we waited for the lock operator to let us through, we rummaged through a compartment on the jet ski and found some candy. We were hungry.

We studied the map on my cell and memorized the landmarks and bridges ahead. When it got dark, we'd need large landmarks to guide us.

We waited about two hours for our turn to pass through the lock because commercial vessels went through first. By then, the sun had set. We had no lights on the jet ski.

We turned off the jet ski in the lock. Someone above threw us a line to hang onto so we would stay put as we were lowered down.

We were lowered only an inch or so. It was a nearly imperceptible drop.

Geez, we waited all that time for that?

The High Voltage warning still flashed on the dashboard, and the piercing low-gas alarm kept sounding, too.

"How long could we go?" Susan wondered.

As we moved along slowly, streetlights above reflected

on the river and illuminated our path slightly. Other than the sound of our jet ski engine, it was eerily quiet.

Susan held her iPhone and we followed the blue dot on the map app. We knew we had to pass under three bridges.

The first one went smoothly. But as we approached the next one, we noticed something the map hadn't shown us: There was a drawbridge only a few feet above the water.

We called the marine radio to ask someone to raise it.

No one answered.

We called the lock keeper, who had just helped us through the lock.

No one answered.

We yelled and screamed, hoping someone on the bridge would hear us.

No one answered.

Susan waved her iPhone flashlight, trying to get someone's attention.

No one answered.

The current was strong and pushed us backward. We tried to paddle, but we couldn't fight the current. So we hung onto a railing at the side of the river about 15 feet from the bridge.

"Bill, I think we can get under it," Susan said.

"Too low," I said.

"No, I think we can," Susan insisted. "We have to try. We can't just sit here all night."

She was worried about becoming snack food for lurking alligators.

So we motored to the bridge and I leaned forward on the seat. Susan leaned down behind me.

We turned off the engine and grabbed the bridge support beams above our heads. Slowly, we began pulling ourselves underneath, one beam at a time. We pulled hard to fight the current.

It was dark. Creepy. We tried not to think about what our hands were touching or if there were alligators nearby.

Hand-over-hand we pulled and pulled and pulled.

Then, we saw sky. We made it to the other side!

"You're a freaking genius!" I told Susan and gave her a high-five.

We rubbed the side of the jet ski for good luck and then pushed the ignition button, hoping desperately it would start. Slowly, the motor turned over and started.

We continued to track our progress toward the marina on Susan's iPhone. We saw bright lights in the distance but weren't sure if they were from a barge, a bridge or a marina.

Unfortunately, we soon discovered the lights came from another draw bridge with train tracks. As we got closer, it looked even lower on the water than the last one.

Susan flashed her iPhone light and I turned on the marine radio to call again.

No one answered.

We yelled and screamed.

No one answered.

Susan waved her iPhone.

No one responded.

It was completely dark now and we didn't want to sit and wait. So we tried to pull ourselves underneath again.

We took our positions and grabbed the large beams and started under.

A train roared by a few feet above our heads. We heard bumps and felt debris falling on us. Yuck!

At one point, I made a quick move and Susan grabbed for me. She thought I was falling in.

"It was terrifying," Susan said. "It was so dark under there."

We were making good progress — until we reached the last few beams of the bridge and the handlebars got stuck.

The current was really strong. I don't know if the river was rising or if the last beams were just lower, but we couldn't get under them.

We only needed to clear about a half-an-inch. Surely we could make it through.

I told Susan to climb up front and lay on one side of the jet ski and I would lay on the other. We hoped that would lower the front end of the jet ski enough to get the handlebars through.

It didn't work.

So we tried pushing up on the beams.

Nothing budged.

Exhausted, we headed back to where we started.

We yelled again.

No one answered.

Susan held her iPhone up to the bridge and we could see a phone number. She was too nervous and tired and couldn't remember the whole number.

So she asked me to remember half of it.

The phone was our lifeline and it was dying quickly. It only had 4 percent battery life left. Susan was panicked. Her hands shook.

She finally entered the whole number and let it ring and ring and ring.

It rang about 40 times before someone finally picked up.

"Raise the bridge now!" Susan screamed into the phone. "We are on jet skis, on the river, and are almost out of gas! Raise the bridge!"

"What?!" the voice on the other end said, clearly startled.

It was the bridge operator. He said it would take a few minutes to back the train up and off the bridge before he could let us through.

Strawberry Wine

Jennifer and Jackie were in New Orleans, waiting and worried.

"That was one time on the trip that I was glad I wasn't alone in the Jeep," Jackie said.

Cell phone reception was terrible on the river that day. We weren't able to communicate with the girls for hours.

"Me and my sister were terrified," Jackie said. "We were both in tears. We were worried about the lightning, the rain and them running out of gas."

The girls waited in New Orleans almost all day for us, driving around and trying to find a ramp.

"I was freakin' out," Jennifer said. "I felt helpless."

She kept repeating to Jackie: "That should be me out there."

They found an RV Park, Pontchartrain Landing, which had a private ramp on the river. They used their charm and good looks to persuade the bartender to let us use it.

The girls waited there for hours, sitting at the bar and listening to music.

A 13-year-old girl sang karaoke: "Strawberry Wine," by Ryan Adams.

"Don't spend too much time on the other side…Let the daylight in…Before you get old and you can't break out of it…"

"She had an amazing voice," Jackie said.

The girls waited and waited and waited, staring out at the river, not knowing if and when we would arrive.

"Looking out into the darkness, you can't even see the river," Jennifer said. "But somehow, we're hoping they're going to be able to find the ramp."

Almost There

Once Susan and I passed under that final drawbridge, we were nearly there.

Maybe we were exhausted and misreading the maps, but we couldn't tell where the ramp was. Plus, the periodic warning beep for our near-empty gas tank unnerved us.

So we went into the first marina we saw and headed toward a light coming from a pleasure boat docked there.

As we got closer, we saw the light came from a television. We pulled up to the dock and I climbed out. (This was the first dock we had seen all day that was low enough for us to climb out!)

I knocked on the boat's window. A woman and man came out, followed by a dog.

We briefly told them our story and they told us theirs: Their son, a double amputee, was kayaking the Mississippi River. Wow!

They were the nicest folks. They gave us some gas and told us the ramp was just around the bend.

As we eased around the corner in the channel, the light from the TV disappeared and we saw nothing but darkness.

Was the ramp on the left? Right?

We chugged along slowly, peering intently into the darkness.

Then, over the sound of the jet ski, we heard whoops and hollers.

Jennifer and Jackie!

Jennifer held up her iPhone and we followed the light.

We docked and climbed off the jet ski onto land. Finally! After nearly 12 hours on the river, we were here!

We hugged. We cried. We laughed. And we got the hell off the river!

After loading the jet ski onto the trailer for the last time, we all climbed into the Jeep.

The girls handed us beers. Susan and I sat in the back seat and cracked 'em open.

No matter how shitty the day had been, at that moment, things couldn't have gotten any better.

Final Chapter

Time to Celebrate and Reflect

"To Captain Bill!"

Clink!

We were at dinner with friends in the French Quarter, and I was being toasted for leading our successful journey down The Big Muddy.

Champagne never tasted so good!

My business partner, Larry, his wife, Marlene, and our friends Beth and Ken Misener were there to celebrate with us.

I felt happy and relaxed. After drinks at Lafitte's Blacksmith Shop Bar and then the Carousel Bar, where the bar turns like a merry-go-round, we enjoyed a fabulous meal at Arnaud's, a nearly 100-year-old restaurant in the heart of New Orleans.

I had no maps to pore over. No problems to solve. No bad weather to anticipate.

I could sit back and enjoy.

Relaxing in Luxury

It had been nearly 24 hours since we completed our harrowing final day on the Mississippi River. We had arrived at the Ritz-Carlton late Friday night, wet, stinky and exhausted.

We celebrated over drinks at the hotel bar before crashing for the night.

Larry had insisted on the luxurious hotel accommodations. He said anyone who completed such a crazy mission deserved some pampering at the end.

So imagine the sight of us — dirty, wet and stinky — pulling up to the valet at the Ritz with two muddy jet skis in tow. Larry gave the valet a heads-up before we arrived.

"He thought it was so cool that this guy took jet skis down the Mississippi that he let Bill park them at the front of the hotel the whole stay," Larry said.

Larry chuckled at my resolve to get the jet ski off the river, which he learned added hours — and lots of anxiety — to our trip that final day.

"I would have just left it in the river," Larry said.

We stayed in New Orleans for the weekend, recuperating, celebrating and reflecting on what we had accomplished.

Many thoughts and lessons learned ran through my mind during that time. They could fill a quote board:

If execution was understood in the planning phase, most missions would be abandoned . . .

The strength of the execution relies on knowledge, creativity and luck.

The journey is different from the plan, despite your best intentions.

Dream. It's what keeps you moving.

I tried to approach this trip in the same way I approach my architecture business: Dream, Plan, Execute, Focus and Celebrate.

I came to realize, especially after my cancer, that the celebrating piece was just as important as the others.

What I didn't realize before this trip was how hard the execution of the journey would be. Not necessarily the physical part of it, although that was difficult.

The toughest part of the river journey was the emotional piece. The same is true of my journey through cancer.

With my cancer, I kind of buried the emotional piece. I didn't think or talk about dying. I acted — as much as I could — as if nothing had changed. I went to work; I drove myself to my treatments. I chit-chatted with my daughters but didn't really talk to them about how they were feeling about my illness.

I should have realized that I couldn't get away with this on the river journey, where we had to keep everyone focused and motivated and work as a team to succeed.

But I didn't anticipate how challenging it would be to deal with everyone's emotions.

Maybe I was naïve. Maybe I was just ignorant.

But what I learned on the trip was that dealing with the team's emotions was critical to the success of our journey. That building a team, creating buy-in, was essential.

And to do that, I had to listen, empathize and (try to) understand.

I reflected a lot on that during our respite in New Orleans. I thought back on the first half of the trip vs. the second. They were so different.

On the first trip, Jackie and Jennifer were kids, teenagers struggling to cope with the fact that their dad had cancer and nearly died. Nancy and I were husband and wife but, as I realized, not true partners.

I treated the girls like kids and Nancy like an unwilling participant.

I was impatient, demanding and not very empathetic. I had 10 days and a mission, and I didn't want anything or anyone getting in my way.

But we didn't succeed because we weren't a team; we were a collection of individuals who were physically together but not emotionally bonded.

On the second trip, my daughters were in their 20s and young adults. They had grown up a lot after dealing with my cancer and weathering the breakup of our family after their mom left.

The trauma of the divorce built a deeper bond between the girls and me, a bond that created a stronger foundation for us. That connection continued to grow during the second leg of the trip.

"I think my dad had a lot more faith in me and my sister on the second trip," Jackie said. "It was really nice, a good feeling."

But it was more than a trust in their abilities. I developed a better understanding of who my daughters are and what they need.

"When we took the first Mississippi trip, my dad and I didn't talk at all about emotional things, like friends do," Jackie said. "Now, when I have trouble with my boyfriend, I can call my dad...

"He's learned how to make me feel better when I'm really struggling."

That understanding developed on the second trip as I listened to Jackie's fears and anxieties and focused on trying to calm them and not dismiss or ignore them.

My relationship with Jennifer grew, too. The night in Vicksburg when she opened up to us about her drug addiction was a huge step toward better understanding and supporting her.

"The physical trip was the least of it," Jennifer said of our journey down the Mississippi. "The relationships, the growth, the challenges, the interpersonal connections. That was what the trip was all about.

"Finishing the river was the initial goal," she said. "But once we started onto the river, that wasn't even it. We were just trying to make it together."

It meant so much to me that Susan was in it together with us.

God, she was on this trip all the way. Never complaining, never quitting.

We got along amazingly. We didn't fight. We didn't blame. It was so different than my experience with Nancy. I tried not to push as hard as the first trip, so I think that helped, too.

If it was a test of our relationship, we passed.

"It wasn't meant to be a test," Susan said, "but afterward, when I look back on it, it was pretty important to find out that in times of severe stress, Bill is someone who stays calm...

"There was never one ugly word from him, which just amazed me. He never lost his temper. ... and not once did Bill or I blame the other. It was just, 'How do we get through this?'

"That's what I learned about Bill on this trip: When he sets a goal, he's going to do it. He perseveres. It was important for me to see that in him, that strength of character."

My daughters say they saw a similar determination in me.

"I saw his work ethic in our journey down the Mississippi," Jennifer said. "Before this trip, I had never seen such determination."

And that changed their view of me—and our relationship.

"Spending this time with my Dad on the Mississippi ... without that we would definitely not have the same relationship," Jennifer said.

"Before, there was significantly less respect for him, in general," Jennifer said. "Afterward, I had exponentially more respect. I knew more about him; I experienced more about him."

I was proud of my daughters' perseverance, too. I always knew they were strong. I wanted them to believe it, too.

"The Mississippi trip made me realize how strong I am, how strong we all are," Jackie said. "I didn't realize how big of a deal it was until afterward. It's definitely made me a stronger person."

Jennifer, too, found great meaning in our journey together.

"Finishing the trip was huge," Jennifer said. "For me, it was symbolic of all of the other shit we had to go through. The real journey with all of us."

That was supposed to be the end of the story — and the end of this book. But on February 25, 2016, Jennifer died of a drug overdose — a loss that has been deep and painful beyond what I have ever experienced.

So now I am on a new journey to healing. My toughest yet.

When I visit Jennifer now, there are no new memories for her to share with me and no new struggles and challenges of daily life to talk about. But as I listen closely, I hear her infectious laugh that was so much fun to be around and feel the hope Jennifer always held in her heart. And it inspires me.

That's why I decided to launch the Emerald Jenny Foundation to help others with addiction.

Jennifer's addiction did not define her, and her memory will live on to aid others. This book is for you, my dear co-pilot, friend and lovely daughter, Jennifer Emerald Ayars.

SOURCES

Chapter 1
www.PBS.org
www.dnr.mo.gov
www.dnr.mo.gov/education/bigriver/mississippi-river/how-locks-and-dams-work.pdf

Chapter 3
www.Biography.com

Chapter 5
www.fws.gov/chickasaw
www.water.epa.gov/type/wetlands/bottomland.cfm
www.accuweather.com

Chapter 6
U.S. Census Bureau

Chapter 7
www.greatriverroad.com
www.nps.gov/miss/riverfacts.htm
www.greenvillems.org and www.visitgreenville.org
www.history.com

Chapter 8
Mississippi Blues Commission
www.cedargroveinn.com
www.greatriverroad.com
Vicksburg Convention and Visitor's Bureau
The Boston Globe, Sept. 8, 2012
Vicksburg Post/The Boston Globe

Chapter 9

www.cityofnatchez.net
www.visitnatchez.org
www.magnoliagrill.com
www.monmouthhistoricinn.com

Chapter 10

Wikipedia, Red River Campaign

Acknowledgments

This book couldn't have happened without my daughters, Jennifer and Jackie, whose strength and support made my journey down The Big Muddy possible. I'd also like to thank my lovely girlfriend, Susan Mills Tarry, for her strength and courage on our trip and her love always.

I am forever grateful to my parents, Dean Curtis Ayars (1919-2009) and Mary Ellen Ayars (1922-2013), and my brothers and sisters — Dean Ayars, Patricia Hinds and Nancy Blatt — and their families.

I also want to thank my incredible medical team, starting with my family doctor, Dr. John Victor Wirtz, who took the original X-ray that detected my tumor. In addition, I am grateful to the following experts at the Cleveland Clinic and the Cleveland Clinic Fairview Hospital Moll Cancer Pavilion:
- Dr. Hamed Daw, my primary oncologist.
- Dr. Kevin Kerwin, the doctor who took charge when clots were discovered on August 3, 2006, and whom I saw again at my last chemo treatment in December 2006.
- All the physicians and staff at Fairview Hospital who diagnosed, treated and cared for me.

Finally, I want to acknowledge the support and encouragement of my friends and business partners, including:
- Larry Fischer, co-founder of Perspectus Architecture.
- Dr. Curtis Rimmerman, a classmate and friend at Case Western Reserve University's Executive MBA program. His assistance throughout my cancer diagnosis and treatment gave me comfort and guidance.
- Everyone at Perspectus Architecture.
- Mike Lizert for making the initial $1 bet.
- Everyone who donated to the fundraiser.

Bill Ayars